# The Mind of the Strategist

# The Mind of the Strategist

## The Art of Japanese Business

## Kenichi Ohmae
*Director, McKinsey & Company, Inc.*

## McGraw-Hill Book Company

New York   St. Louis   San Francisco   Auckland
Bogotá   Hamburg   Johannesburg   London   Madrid
Mexico   Montreal   New Delhi   Panama   Paris
São Paulo   Singapore   Sydney   Tokyo   Toronto

**Library of Congress Cataloging in Publication Data**
Ohmae, Kenichi.
  The mind of the strategist.

  Includes index.
  1. Industrial management.   2. Industrial management—Japan.   3. Strategy.   I. Title.
HD38.0315        658.4'012        81–18630
ISBN  0–07–047595–4              AACR2

ISBN 0-07-047595-4

The editors for this book were William Newton and Eric Lowen-
kron, the designer was Mark E. Safran, and the production supervisor was Teresa F. Leaden. It was set in Century Schoolbook by
Datapage.

Printed and bound by The Murray Printing Company.

*For Marvin Bower, my role model, with admiration: and for Jeannie, Soki and Hiroki, my family, with love.*

# About the Author

As an adviser to top management, author, and speaker, Kenichi Ohmae has been described as "Mr. Strategy" in his native Japan, where he heads the office of McKinsey & Company, the international consulting firm. Some of Japan's most famous and internationally successful companies regularly seek his help in shaping their competitive strategies, and his counsel is likewise much in demand among U.S.- and European-based multinationals.

As a director of McKinsey & Company and co-leader of its strategic management practice, Ohmae has served companies in a wide spectrum of industries: industrial and consumer electronics, office equipment, photographic equipment, industrial machinery, food, rubber, and chemicals. His special interest and area of expertise is formulating creative strategies and developing organizational concepts to implement them.

During the past six years Ohmae has produced five books on strategy (three of them runaway best-sellers in Japan) and more than twenty-five articles on strategy-related topics as well as several other books on various aspects of Japanese culture. Besides scientific papers in the *Journal of Nuclear Engineering* and the *Journal of Nuclear Materials* (he holds a Ph.D. in nuclear engineering from the Massachusetts Institute of Technology), his publications in English include articles in *Chief Executive, European Management,* and *The McKinsey Quarterly*. This is his first book to be published in English.

Born in 1943 on the island of Kyushu, Kenichi Ohmae

now makes his home in Yokohama with his wife, Jeannette, and their children, Soki and Hiroki. His spare-time interests include music (he is an accomplished clarinetist), sailing, and scuba diving.

# Contents

# Foreword

This is an important book for top executives and others concerned with the subject of strategic planning. Its Japanese origins alone make it worthy of consideration.

In the past two years, American business readers have been deluged with scores of books and articles purporting to unlock the secrets of Japan's global business success. The "keys" supplied by the authors of these treatises make an imposing bundle: consensus decision making, lifetime employment, "Japan, Inc.," a "shame" culture, longer planning horizons, *kanban* production systems, quality circles, Zen Buddhism—you name it. Each of these affords some measure of insight. But until now, none has unlocked the central enigma.

Has Kenichi Ohmae done so in this book? Although my company, PepsiCo, Inc., has a significant involvement in several major Japanese industries (e.g., soft drinks, snacks, and restaurants), I cannot judge with certainty.

But I am convinced that Ohmae has come very close to the heart of the matter. He has done so not by explaining the whys and wherefores of Japanese business prowess (although the book is full of fascinating case examples) but simply by enabling the reader to look through the eyes, and think with the mind, of an extraordinarily talented Japanese business strategist. Ohmae is not a journalist or an academic; he is an active professional strategist with a clientele that includes some of the world's largest and most sophisticated companies and an unmatched reputation as a consultant and author in Japan. He has hands-on experience in helping to fashion winning corporate strategies.

Ohmae's book contains many original and provocative insights. Yet for all its substance and subtlety, it is genuinely easy reading—simple and personal in tone, lucid and logical in style. It is, in fact, not an easy book to put down. At the same time, most of the chapters are self-contained and can be read separately. This is a book you can come back to.

One of Ohmae's most valuable contributions is that his book is focused more on the substance of strategic planning than on the form. Thus, the reader can learn how a strategist goes about generating a real competitive edge, not just what to cover in strategy exercises. This special focus makes the book worthwhile reading for the chief executive as well as for line managers.

Not all the ideas in these pages are new. After all, this is a book on fundamentals. But fundamentals as Ohmae expresses them are worth reexamination, and not only because they are seen in a distinctive context. In my experience, it is the fundamentals that too often get overlooked by corporate strategists. It is no small part of Ohmae's accomplishment that he is able to present them with a freshness that conveys something of the excitement of discovery.

The directness and acuity of this strategist's mind come through on every page of the book, which combines depth and power with refreshing simplicity. To be sure, the businessman who reads it only to find out "how the Japanese do it" will be rewarded with a rich harvest of facts and insights. But the reader who wants to develop planning skills—to learn how to focus on generating real competitive ideas—will find the book remarkably stimulating. This is what gives *The Mind of the Strategist* unique and universal worth.

**Andrall E. Pearson**
*President*
*PepsiCo, Inc.*

# The Mind of the
# Strategist

# Introduction

As a management consultant employed by an international consulting firm, I travel widely and talk with hundreds of senior executives in Europe, North America, and Asia. Almost without exception, I find that these business leaders, many of them older and far wiser than I, are keenly interested in what I have to say about business strategy. The reason is quite simple: I happen to be Japanese.

Everyone thinks the Japanese possess some special magic that enables them to run rings around their competitors in world markets. As a Western-educated Japanese who knows the Japanese business world intimately but can speak the language of Western business leaders, I must—or so they seem to think—possess some measure of that magic. And I might, just possibly, be prepared to whisper the secret formula into their waiting ears.

Of course I am exaggerating. None of the businessmen I talk to really thinks that there is any kind of secret formula behind the performance of Japanese business in world competition. But they are dissatisfied with the glib explanations for that performance that have been so freely offered on television and in the press by many so-called experts on the Japanese way of business life. They are convinced that there must be more to it than "Japan, Inc.," consensus decision making, company songs, and quality circles. And they are right.

Except in a peripheral way, the insights from Japan that I may be able to offer my friends and readers on

Western business have little if anything to do with formulas and techniques. As a consultant I have had the opportunity to work with many large Japanese companies. Among them are many companies whose success you would say must be the result of superb strategies. But when you look more closely, you discover a paradox. They have no big planning staffs, no elaborate, gold-plated strategic planning processes. Some of them are painfully handicapped by lack of the resources—people, money, and technology—that seemingly would be needed to implement an ambitious strategy. Yet despite all these handicaps, they are outstanding performers in the marketplace. Year after year, they manage to build share and create wealth.

How do they do it? The answer is easy. They may not have a strategic planning staff, but they do have a strategist of great natural talent: usually the founder or chief executive. Often—especially in Japan, where there is no business school—these outstanding strategists have had little or no formal business education, at least at the college level. They may never have taken a course or read a book on strategy. But they have an intuitive grasp of the basic elements of strategy. They have an idiosyncratic mode of thinking in which company, customers, and competition merge in a dynamic interaction out of which a comprehensive set of objectives and plans for action eventually crystallizes.

Insight is the key to this process. Because it is creative, partly intuitive, and often disruptive of the status quo, the resulting plans might not even hold water from the analyst's point of view. It is the creative element in these plans and the drive and will of the mind that conceived them that give these strategies their extraordinary competitive impact.

Both in Japan and in the West, this breed of natural or instinctive strategist is dying out or at least being pushed to the sidelines in favor of rational, by-the-numbers strategic and financial planners. Today's giant institutions, both public and private, are by and large not organized for innovation. Their systems and processes are all oriented toward incremental improvement—doing better what they are doing already. In the United States, the pressure of innumerable social and governmental constraints on corporate activities—most notably, perhaps, the proliferation of government regulations during the 1960s and 1970s—has put a premium on the talent for adaptation and reduced still further the incentive to innovate. Advocates of bold and ambitious strategies too often find themselves on the sidelines, labeled as losers, while the rewards go to those more skilled at working within the system. This is especially true in mature industries, where actions and ideas often move in narrow grooves, forcing out innovators. Conversely, venture capital groups tend to attract the flexible, adaptive minds.

In all times and places, large institutions develop cultures of their own, and success is often closely tied to the ability to conform. In our day, the culture of most business corporations exalts logic and rationality; hence, it is analysts rather than innovators who tend to get ahead. It is not unreasonable to say that many large U.S. corporations today are run like the Soviet economy. In order to survive, they must plan ahead comprehensively, controlling an array of critical functions in every detail. They specify policies and procedures in meticulous detail, spelling out for practically everyone what can and what cannot be done in particular circumstances. They establish hurdle rates, analyze risks, and anticipate contingencies. As strategic planning processes have burgeoned in these companies, strategic thinking has gradually withered away.

My message in this book, as you will have guessed by now, is that successful business strategies result not from rigorous analysis but from a particular state of mind. In what I call the mind of the strategist, insight and a consequent drive for achievement, often amounting to a sense of mission, fuel a thought process which is basically creative and intuitive rather than rational. Strategists do not reject analysis. Indeed they can hardly do without it. But they use it only to stimulate the creative process, to test the ideas that emerge, to work out their strategic implications, or to ensure successful execution of high-potential "wild" ideas that might otherwise never be implemented properly. Great strategies, like great works of art or great scientific discoveries, call for technical mastery in the working out but originate in insights that are beyond the reach of conscious analysis.

If this is so—if the mind of the strategist is so deeply at odds with the culture of the corporation—how can an already institutionalized company recover the capacity to conceive and execute creative business strategies? In a book entitled *The Corporate Strategist* that was published in Japan in 1975, I attempted to answer that question in a specifically Japanese context.

In Japan, a different set of conditions from those in the West inhibits the creation of bold and innovative strategies. In the large Japanese company, promotion is based on tenure; there is no fast track for brilliant performers. No one reaches a senior management post before the mid-fifties, and chief executives are typically over 60—well past the age when they are likely to be able to generate dynamic strategic ideas. At the same time, the inventive, often aggressive younger people have no means of contributing in a significant way to the strategy of the corporation. The result: strategic stagnation or the strong probability of it.

How, I asked myself, could the mind of the strategist, with its inventive élan, be reproduced in this kind of corporate culture? What were the ingredients of an excellent strategist, and how could they be reproduced in the Japanese context? These were the questions I addressed in my book. The answer I came up with involved the formation within the corporation of a group of young "samurais" who would play a dual role. On the one hand they would function as real strategists, giving free rein to their imagination and entrepreneurial flair in order to come up with bold and innovative strategic ideas. On the other hand they would serve as staff analysts, testing out, digesting, and assigning priorities to the ideas, and providing staff assistance to line managers in implementing the approved strategies. This "samurai" concept has since been adopted in several Japanese firms with great success.

Such a solution would not fit the circumstances of the typical American or European company. Yet it seems to me that the central notion of my book and of a sequel published in Japan eighteen months later is relevant to the problem of strategic stagnation in any organization. There are ways in which the mind of the strategist can be reproduced, or simulated, by people who may lack a natural talent for strategy. Putting it another way, although there is no secret formula for inventing a successful strategy, there are some specific concepts and approaches that can help anyone develop the kind of mentality that comes up with superior strategic ideas. Thus the reader will find in this book no formulas for successful business strategy. What I have tried to supply in their place is a series of hints that may help him or her develop the capacity for and the habit of strategic thinking.

It remains to say something about the content and organization of the book. The material on which it is based includes several Japanese publications of mine, including *The Corporate Strategists* (Parts I and II); *McKinsey: Contemporary Strategic Management;* an article, "Effective Strategies for Competitive Success," that originally appeared in *The McKinsey Quarterly;* and a monograph, "The Strategic Triangle," first published in the *McKinsey Staff Papers* series.

In citing my own writings as my sources, I am by no means advancing a claim to have invented or discovered all the strategic concepts the reader will encounter in this book. In one form or another, many of them have been the common intellectual property of informed business people for many years—at least since they were given definitive expression by such scholars as Peter Drucker, Theodore Levitt, Michael Porter, and probably many others. As a doer rather than a reader, I am not well versed in the works of established authorities, yet I cannot have escaped the influence of their ideas. My object in this book, however, has not been to break new theoretical ground but, in a sense, to put theory in its place—a place distinctly secondary to creative intuition in the tool kit of the successful strategist.

As for organization, Part I, "The Art of Strategic Thinking," concentrates on the basics of the mental process. Chapter 1 introduces the process and illustrates its analytical dimension. The next five chapters explore the directions which the strategic thinker may pursue in quest of innovative strategies, and Chapter 7 describes the nature of that pursuit itself.

In Part II the emphasis shifts from process to substance, examining how different kinds of strategies result from focusing on the different points of what I call the strategic triangle: company, customer, and competition. The final chapter of Part II explains corporate strategy, as distinguished from business strategy. Among other things it touches on the controversial concept of product portfolio management, a central tool of present-day strategic planning, and its role in the development of overall corporate strategies.

Part III is concerned mainly with environmental factors bearing on strategic thinking and strategy formulation, with an excursion to the present-day Japanese business scene, an overall perspective on the nature of strategic foresight, and a postscript chapter that summarizes my ideas on the formulation of successful strategy.

Since most of these chapters have been translated in whole or in part from the Japanese and the rest were composed in perhaps rather Japanese-accented English, I must ask the reader to be patient with any eccentricities of style or thought that he or she may encounter. (Speaking of "he or she," this is as good a place as any to emphasize that the consistent use of the masculine pronoun in referring to "the manager," "the planner," "the corporate strategist," and other *dramatis personae* of the book is a matter of grammatical convenience. It is also, in the great majority of cases in Japan, still the more realistic choice.)

It remains for me to thank my many colleagues in McKinsey & Company whose ideas and techniques I have drawn on freely in developing my approach to the problems of strategy discussed in this book. Although their thinking has contributed immeasurably to my own, they are in no way responsible for the uses I have made of it.

Two colleagues in particular have contributed to the development of the text. I am indebted to Max Geldens for his insights and detailed comments on the manuscript. I am also profoundly obligated to Roland Mann for his invaluable contribution as editor, critic, and project manager.

For better or worse, however, the overall approach to business strategy reflected in this book is a very personal one, and responsibility for the many controversial judgments it contains must be mine alone.

# Part 1
# The Art of
# Strategic Thinking

# 1
# Analysis: The Starting Point

Some weeks ago I received a brochure from a Japanese travel agency inviting me to "enjoy sport amid fantastic scenic beauty." The eye-catching headline advertised "golf, tennis, archery, bicycling, sailing—the sport of your choice" in an "ideal vacation spot," the heart of Ise-Shima National Park, famous for its intricate shoreline and its production of cultured pearls.

Having once worked as a tour guide, I knew how exhausting an all-day trip from Tokyo to the Shima Peninsula can be; but the pamphlet intrigued me.

The schedule was strenuous. The bus was to leave Tokyo at 9 a.m. on Saturday, arriving at the vacation hotel at 5 p.m. after a journey of more than 200 miles. The next morning, there would be time for the sports the pamphlet touted. Then, at 2:30 p.m., the bus would leave for Tokyo, arriving at 10:30 p.m. Sunday night.

It looked to me as if the time available for enjoying the beauties of nature described in the brochure—"majestic green ridges linking mountain to mountain," "clear cobalt-blue skies," "the azure sea," and "picturesque small bays dotted with pearl rafts"—was likely to be rather short. My pocket calculator confirmed that nearly 43 percent of the excursion period would be spent riding in the bus. Sleeping, eating, bathing, dressing, and so on, which one can (and will) do at home anyway, would take up another 40 percent. That would leave 6½ hours, or a mere 17 percent, for the sports which were supposed to be the object of the trip. The cost quoted was $125, which would work out to approximately $19.25 per hour of sport. If it was tennis I had in mind, I would clearly do a lot better to take a half-hour drive out to some public tennis club in a Tokyo suburb, pay a fee of $12, and enjoy myself there for the day.

What the travel agency was selling, of course, was a package consisting of a number of different elements, including "atmosphere," integrated into a whole. Customers normally pay their $125 for the package without trying to identify precisely how much they are paying for each element and whether it is all really worth the cost. To do this, one has to probe into what is actually being offered, disentangling the various components of the package and understanding how each element contributes to the whole.

Returning to my example, it is clear that as far as the sport alone is concerned, a tennis player would get 10 times the value by staying in the city and playing on a local court. But having recognized that, suppose you love to play tennis in a spectacular scenic setting, and you've been longing to see the well-advertised beauties of Ise-Shima National Park. In that case, do these secondary considerations justify the expense after all? They might, or they might not. The point is that analysis has enabled you to substitute your own *self-directed* judgment for the *other-directed* way of accepting the package—paying for an atmosphere you haven't even tried to define.

Analysis is the critical starting point of strategic thinking. Faced with problems, trends, events, or situations that appear to constitute a harmonious whole or come packaged as a whole by the common sense of the day, the strategic thinker dissects them into their constituent parts. Then, having discovered the significance of these constituents, he reassembles them in a way calculated to maximize his advantage.

In business as on the battlefield, the object of strategy is to bring about the conditions most favorable to one's own side, judging precisely the right moment to attack or withdraw and always assessing the limits of compromise correctly. Besides the habit of analysis, what marks the mind of the strategist is an intellectual elasticity or flexibility that enables him to come up with realistic responses to changing situations, not simply to discriminate with great precision among different shades of gray.

In strategic thinking, one first seeks a clear understanding of the particular character of each element of a situation and then makes the fullest possible use of human brainpower to restructure the elements in the most advantageous way. Phenomena and events in the real world do not always fit a linear model. Hence the most reliable means of dissecting a situation into its constituent parts and reassembling them in the desired pattern is not a step-by-step methodology such as systems analysis. Rather, it is that ultimate nonlinear thinking tool, the human brain. True strategic thinking thus contrasts sharply with the conventional mechanical systems approach based on linear thinking. But it also contrasts with the approach that stakes everything on intuition, reaching conclusions without any real breakdown or analysis (Figure 1–1).

No matter how difficult or unprecedented the problem, a breakthrough to the best possible solution can come only from a combination of rational analysis, based on

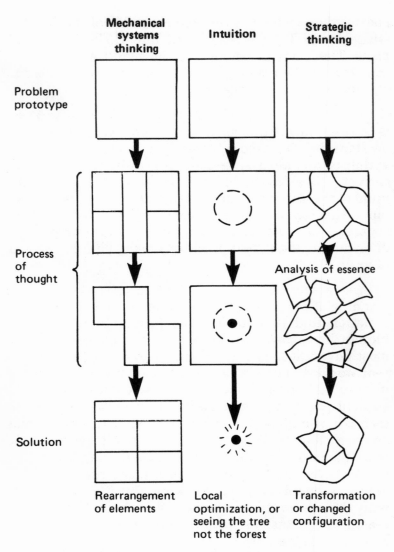

**Figure 1-1**  Three kinds of thinking process.

the real nature of things, and imaginative reintegration of all the different items into a new pattern, using nonlinear brainpower. This is always the most effective approach to devising strategies for dealing successfully with challenges and opportunities, in the market arena as on the battlefield.

## Determining the critical issue

The first stage in strategic thinking is to pinpoint the critical issue in the situation. Everyone facing a problem naturally tries in his or her own way to penetrate to the key issue. Some may think that one way is as good as another and that whether their efforts hit the mark is largely a matter of luck. I believe it is not a question of luck at all but of attitude and method. In problem solving, it is vital at the start to formulate the question in a way that will facilitate the discovery of a solution.

Suppose, for example, that overtime work has become chronic in a company, dragging down profitability. If we frame the question as: What should be done to reduce overtime? many answers will suggest themselves:

¶ Work harder during the regular working hours

¶ Shorten the lunch period and coffee breaks

¶ Forbid long private telephone conversations

Such questioning is often employed by companies trying to lower costs and improve product quality by using zero defect campaigns and quality control (QC) circles that involve the participation of all employees. Ideas are gathered, screened, and later incorporated in the improvement program. But this approach has an intrinsic limitation. *The questions are not framed to point toward a solution; rather, they are directed toward finding reme-dies to symptoms.*

Returning to our overtime problem, suppose we frame the question in a more solution-oriented way: Is this company's work force large enough to do all the work required?

To this question there can be only one of two answers—yes or no. To arrive at the answer yes, a great deal of analysis would be needed, probably including a comparison with other companies in the same industries, the historical trend of workload per employee, and the degree of automation and computerization and their economic effectiveness. On the other hand, if—after careful perusal of the sales record, profit per employee, ratio between direct and indirect labor, comparison with other companies, and so on—the answer should turn out to be no (i.e., the company is currently understaffed), this in itself would be tantamount to a solution of the original problem. This solution—an increase in personnel—will be validated by all the usual management indicators. And if the company adopts this solution, the probability increases that the desired outcome will actually follow. This way, objective analysis can supplant emotional discussions.

That is not the only way the question could have been formulated, however. We might have asked it this way: Do the capabilities of the employees match the nature of the work?

This formulation, like the previous one, is oriented toward deriving a possible solution. Here too, a negative answer would imply a shortage of suitable personnel, which would in turn suggest that the solution should be sought either in staff training or in recruiting capable staff from elsewhere. On the other hand, if the answer is yes, this indicates that the problem of chronic overtime lies not in the nature of the work but in the amount of the workload. Thus, not training but adding to the work force would then be the crucial factor in the solution.

If the right questions are asked in a solution-oriented manner, and if the proper analyses are carried out, the final answer is likely to be the same, even though it may have started from a differently phrased question and may have been arrived at by a different route. In either case, a question concerning the nature and amount of work brings the real issue into focus and makes it easy to arrive at a clear-cut verdict.

It is hard to overstate the importance of formulating the question correctly. People who are trained and motivated to formulate the right questions will not offer vague proposals for "improvements," as are seen in many suggestion boxes. They will come up with concrete, practical ideas.

By failing to grasp the critical issues, too many senior managers today impose great anxiety on themselves and their subordinates, whose efforts end in failure and frustration. Solution-oriented questions can be formulated only if the critical issue is localized and grasped accurately in the first place. A clear common understanding of the nature of a problem that has already been localized provides a critical pressure to come up with creative solutions. When problems are poorly defined or vaguely comprehended, one's creative mind does not work sharply. The greater one's tolerance for lukewarm solutions, half measures, and what the British used to call muddling through, the more loosely the issue is likely to be defined. For this reason, isolating the crucial points of the problem—in other words, determining the critical issue —is most important to the discovery of a solution. The

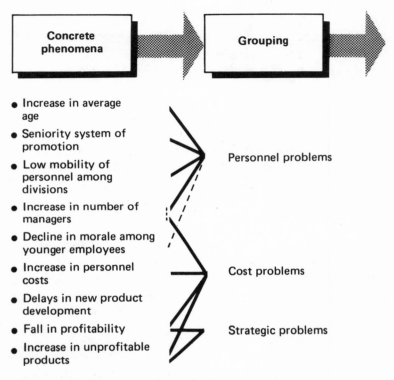

**Figure 1-2** Narrowing down the issue.

key at this initial stage is to *narrow down the issue by studying the observed phenomena closely.*

Figure 1–2 illustrates one method often used by strategists in the process of *abstraction,* showing how it might work in the case of a large, established company faced with the problem of declining competitive vigor.

The first step in the abstraction process is to use such means as brainstorming and opinion polls to assemble and itemize the respects in which the company is at a disadvantage vis-à-vis its competitors. These points can

| Abstraction | Determination of approach (very concrete and specific) |

Inflexibility in
organization

Plan for
reorganization

Costs high compared
with competitors

Plan for improving
profitability

Inflexibility in corporate
strategy

Revised strategic
approach

then be classified under a smaller number of headings (shown in the exhibit as Concrete Phenomena) according to their common factors.

Next, phenomena sharing some common denominator are themselves combined into groups. Having done this, we look once again at each group as a unit and ask ourselves what crucial issue each unit poses. The source of the problem must be understood before any real solution can be found, and the process of abstraction enables us to bring the crucial issues to light without the risk of overlooking anything important.

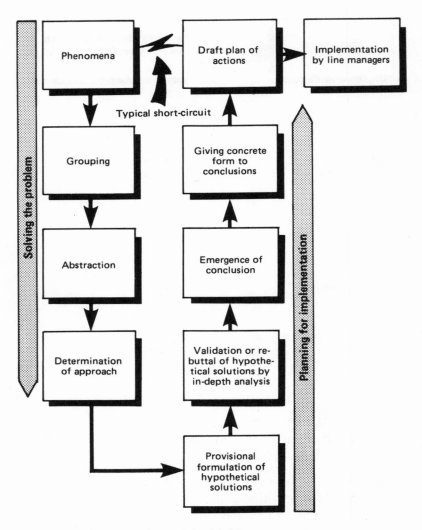

**Figure 1–3** Stages of strategic thinking.

Once the abstraction process has been completed, we must next decide on the right approach to finding a solution. Once we have determined the solution in principle,

THE ART OF STRATEGIC THINKING

there remains the task of working out implementation programs and then compiling detailed action plans. No solution, however perfectly it may address the critical issue, can be of the slightest use until it is implemented. Too many companies try to short-circuit the necessary steps between identification of critical issues and line implementation of solutions by skipping the intermediate steps: planning for operational improvement and organizing for concrete actions. Even the most brilliant line manager cannot translate an abstract plan into action in a single step.

Later we shall look at examples of the intermediate steps in more detail. For the time being it will suffice to remember that the process pictured in Figure 1–3—abstraction followed by movement toward a concrete plan for improvement—is characteristic of the method of solution finding that focuses on critical issues.

### Fail-safe methodology

Suppose we have only a general idea of what the critical issue may be in a problem. How can we pinpoint it without wasting time? People with a genius for ferreting out the critical issue by instinct are rare. Fortunately for the rest of us, it can also be done by method.

The issue diagram is a device familiar to those with experience in computer programming or using decision trees for decision making. The overall problem or issue is divided into two or more mutually exclusive and collectively exhaustive subissues; then the process is repeated for emergent subissues, and so on, until a level is reached at which the subitems are individually manageable. In this way, even a problem that originally seemed too large to cope with will gradually be broken down into a whole series of smaller issues. The secret here is that each of the final items must be something that can be managed by human effort, and the results should be definite and measurable.

Consider the case of a company whose Product A has been showing a steep decline in competitiveness because of high costs. Costs must be lowered, but how? Historical developments and changes in the environment of the company and in Product A will determine the answer to that question.

**The issue diagram.** Rather than recklessly attempting to come up with a solution simply on the basis of experience or intuition, without analyzing these objective factors, the strategic thinker would take a blank sheet of paper and draw up an issue diagram (Figure 1–4). The reasoning would go something like this:

When the manufacturing costs of Product A are too high, the first thing to look at is its design. If the product is manufactured to existing specifications and is already too costly to be competitive, it is obviously overdesigned. But this does not necessarily mean that we ought to alter the design without further ado. Before doing that, we must study the basic needs and tastes of our customers and then estimate how much market share we would be likely to lose to the competition and what the net impact on our profits would be if we were to sell the overdesigned Product A at a higher price, reflecting its actual manufacturing cost.

If we are confident that Product A can earn more than enough to break even in such a contracted market, our next move is likely to be in the marketing area. For example, we might launch a major advertising campaign to persuade the pertinent customer segment that Product A represents premium quality at a premium price. (Volvo, Porsche, and Mercedes-Benz price and sell their cars in this manner, successfully passing on the "high" element of their production costs to the customers.)

But suppose that for reasons of consistent pricing policy or smaller market size we cannot pass the high cost of Product A on to the customer. In this case, the appropriate move would probably be to have recourse to value analysis (VA) and value engineering (VE). The purpose of these techniques, which are now employed by practically every Japanese manufacturer as a part of the routine control of business operations, is to investigate and analyze purchased materials or components from the point of view of price so that the results can be incorporated into planning in such areas as cost reduction and development of new products. Studies of purchased goods are carried out to examine whether their quality and reliability are right for a particular product design and function (value engineering) and whether their costs are reasonable for the product price (value analysis). Production processes, cost structure, and suppliers are examined similarly.

Returning to our example, assume that a thorough study of the trade-off between design costs and the market requirements leads us to conclude that Product A cannot be profitable on the basis of current design. In this situation, VA and VE can help us bring about the conditions necessary to enable Product A to compete in the market.

Remember that the market is formed by Product A and its competition. No product is sold in the desert or on the moon; manufacturers' prices and the various customer segments they serve are determined in a competitive environment. What if *all* manufacturers in the market are producing similar high-quality products and offering

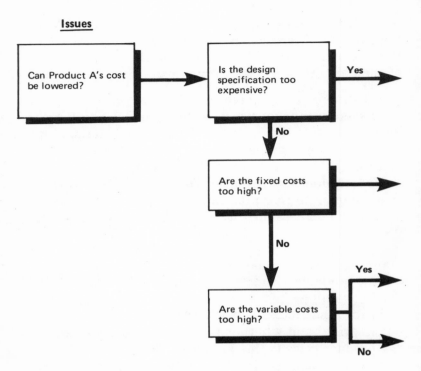

**Issues**

Can Product A's cost be lowered?

Is the design specification too expensive? — Yes →

No ↓

Are the fixed costs too high? →

No ↓

Are the variable costs too high? — Yes →
No →

*Figure 1-4*  A sample issue diagram.

them to the market at a relatively low price (i.e., with narrow profit margins)? In this case, it would be disastrous for the company to modify Product A's design in order to reduce costs—even if, for example, it proved technically feasible to substitute plastic for metal housing—because the resulting seemingly lower quality product would be driven out of the market by the low-priced, high-quality products already competing for the customer's favor.

VA and VE techniques, then, cannot be employed safely in a vacuum. By the same token, designers can't afford to withdraw to an ivory tower and dream up cost-saving

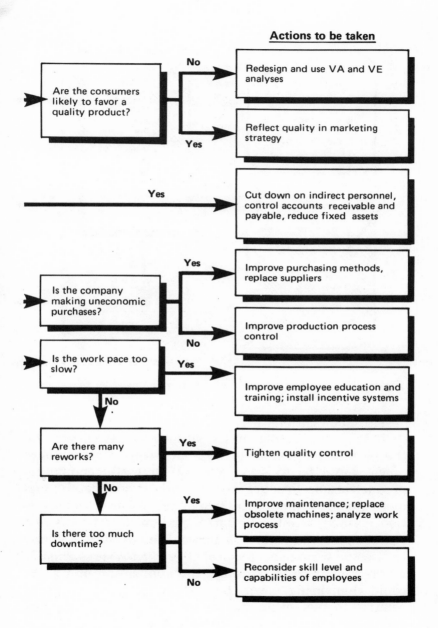

**Actions to be taken**

Are the consumers likely to favor a quality product?
- **No** → Redesign and use VA and VE analyses
- **Yes** → Reflect quality in marketing strategy

**Yes** → Cut down on indirect personnel, control accounts receivable and payable, reduce fixed assets

Is the company making uneconomic purchases?
- **Yes** → Improve purchasing methods, replace suppliers
- **No** → Improve production process control

Is the work pace too slow?
- **Yes** → Improve employee education and training; install incentive systems
- **No** ↓

Are there many reworks?
- **Yes** → Tighten quality control
- **No** ↓

Is there too much downtime?
- **Yes** → Improve maintenance; replace obsolete machines; analyze work process
- **No** → Reconsider skill level and capabilities of employees

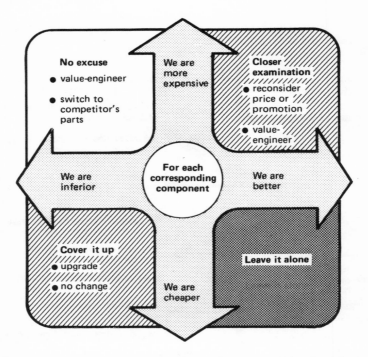

*Figure 1–5* Product-change options after competitive tear-down.

design modifications without reference to what is going on in the marketplace. In the situation I have described, the best way to come up with an effective competitive move would be to set the most successful competing product beside Product A, dismantle it completely, and meticulously compare the two in every aspect: construction method, number of parts, quality of materials and components, and so forth. This would enable the company to discover what part or aspect of Product A is responsible for its higher costs. Through the application of VE, we could then bring down the cost of this part or aspect relative to that of its competitor without imposing any competitive handicap on Product A in the marketplace (Figure 1–5).

At the same time, however, our investigation might have shown that even though the costs of Product A are higher overall, the competing product was made from better-quality materials or had a better finish. In that case, we might need to improve the materials specification or design of Product A and accept the higher costs.

I have digressed somewhat, but for a reason. In many companies today, functional activities such as design, manufacturing, and sales, which are usually divided from one another organizationally, devote more energy to guarding their own territories than to looking for ways to cooperate. As a result the full potential for major profit improvement that typically lies in the interfunctional border areas tends to be overlooked. VA and VE are cited here as examples of forcing devices for analyzing these border areas. VA and VE are normally used by a group of engineers as an internal device to streamline design, but if used in the broader sense as described above, they become a powerful tool to reduce product cost.

In recent years, some advanced companies in Japan pushed this concept even further, challenging the status quo by designing both product and production facility from a zero base, given a specified concept of a product for a well-defined target customer group. This kind of approach—zero-based production and value design (or design from scratch to the standard the user is willing to accept)—is the basis of the success of Honda's Civic and Ricoh's copiers, to name two representative examples.

Let us look once again at Figure 1–4. When we suspect that variable costs are too high and carry our analysis further on the issue diagram, we see that the action required could be either shop-floor training or improved purchasing methods. Jumping from the symptom "variable costs" to a diagnosis of "high cost of goods purchased"

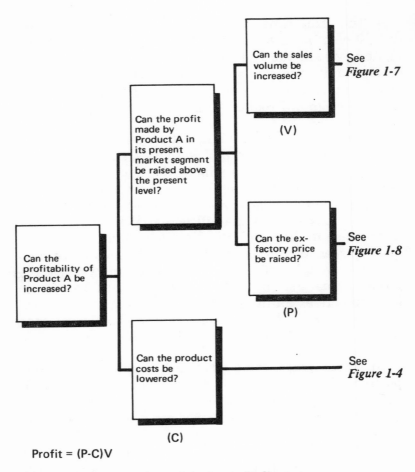

Profit = (P-C)V

*Figure 1–6* The starting point of a profit diagram.

and then implementing measures based on that diagnosis would only lower our chances of correcting the problem.

As I mentioned earlier, this process of narrowing a problem down by means of an issue diagram resembles the methods used in computer programming and decision trees. Alternatively, we can compare it to the process by

THE ART OF STRATEGIC THINKING

which a doctor questions a patient in order to arrive at a diagnosis, sequentially eliminating certain areas of irrelevance. A business enterprise is an organic, living entity. When disease attacks some part of it, the malfunction is bound to be reflected in a reduction of the profit (or future profit potential) that is the energy source of the organism's growth. If they recognize the gravity of the symptoms, the company's top management, either on their own or with the aid of outside consultants, will naturally want to probe for the cause of the problem, just as a doctor questions a patient to find out what is wrong.

**The profit diagram.** Starting from the assumption that the costs of a given product are too high, the issue diagram gives us, as we have just seen, a tool for analyzing the possible reasons. But suppose it has not yet been established that high product costs are in fact the problem; all we know for certain is that selling Product A in the existing market by present sales methods is proving unprofitable. To diagnose this phenomenon, we must move back slightly closer to fundamentals.

This time we start from the question, To what extent can Product A's profitability be improved? Since profit is determined by selling price, cost, and sales volume, all three variables must be given equal weight in the initial stages of a diagnosis aimed at improving profitability.

Not long ago a machine-tool company sought my advice on how to improve the profitability of certain products in its line. As the initial step in the project, I drew up the diagrams set out in Figures 1–6 to 1–8. Because these diagrams apply to most products and are directly related to profit, which is the basis of all business, I call them profit diagrams. We can use them to advantage in the case of Product A.

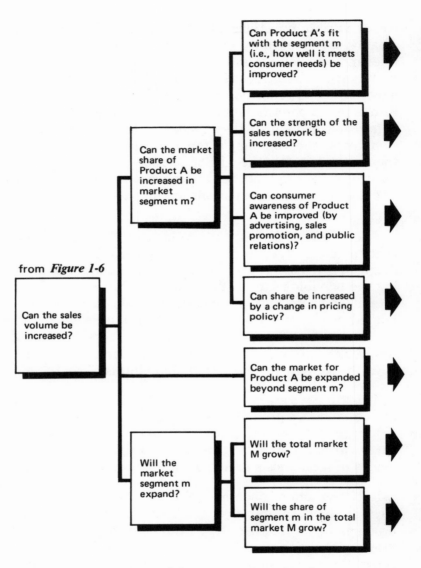

*Figure 1-7* Profit diagram for increasing market share.

THE ART OF STRATEGIC THINKING

### Sample items requiring analysis

- Basic consumer needs
- Analysis of value (real and perceived) offered by competing products

- Trends in sales channel and geographical coverage
- Comparison of servicing capability, delivery time

- Survey of customer awareness in brand and product
- Analysis of purchasing decision-making process

- Price elasticity
- Influence of payment terms and trade-in conditions

- Possibility of geographical expansion
- Possibility of expansion in final customers outside the segment
- Cost-benefit analysis of expansion

- Anticipated demand (3-5 years ahead) for product constituting the total market M

- Factors determining the size of segment m within the market M
- Trends and forecasts of factors above

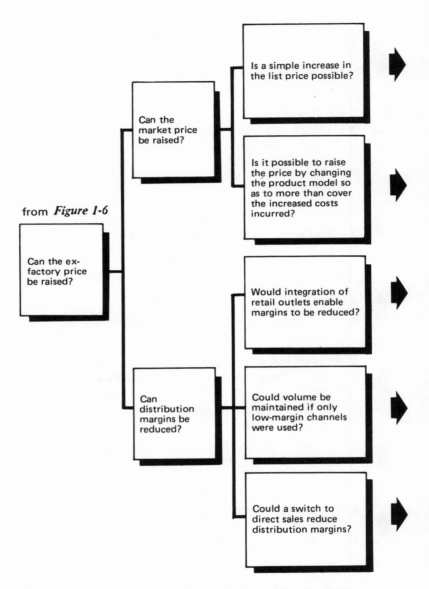

from *Figure 1-6*

Can the ex-factory price be raised?

Can the market price be raised?

Is a simple increase in the list price possible?

Is it possible to raise the price by changing the product model so as to more than cover the increased costs incurred?

Can distribution margins be reduced?

Would integration of retail outlets enable margins to be reduced?

Could volume be maintained if only low-margin channels were used?

Could a switch to direct sales reduce distribution margins?

*Figure 1–8*  Profit diagram for analyzing pricing flexibility.

THE ART OF STRATEGIC THINKING

- Price elasticity
- Possibility of price rises differentiated by geographical areas, models, or by distribution channels
- Results achieved by competitors (possibility of "follow-the-leader" price increase)

- Basic consumer needs in each market segment
- Price elasticity
- Cost-benefit analysis

- Basic economic analysis of distribution system
- Analysis on economies of scale
- Correlation between number of sales outlets and market coverage

- Flexibility in physical flow of goods by distribution channels
- Degree of motivation and sales efforts exerted by different channels

- Analysis of long-term strategic effect
- Analysis of short-term cost-benefit
- Possibility of maintenance of sales skills

Two basic issues are involved in increasing the profitability of Product A.

¶ Can more profit be gained *externally* (i.e., from the market)?

¶ Can product profitability be improved at the present selling price by raising efficiency *internally* (i.e., through cost reduction)?

The first issue can be further divided, as Figure 1–6 shows, into two subissues.

¶ Can sales volume be increased?

¶ Can the price be raised?

In order to find the answers to these questions, more detailed analysis is needed, as shown in Figures 1–7 and 1–8. On the right-hand side of both these exhibits I have given some examples of the analyses required by the issues as posed.

Each type of analysis requires considerable skill and experience and can be undertaken seriously only when there is constant access to accurate market information. Companies that are strong in marketing gather market information at regular intervals so that they can carry out these analyses routinely. Companies that are less marketing-minded and tend to collect information haphazardly are not so fortunate. If they are to carry out each analysis with any prospect of reliable results, they will need to make an extra effort to fill the gaps in the flow of market data they receive.

No proper business strategy can be built on fragmentary knowledge or analysis. If such a strategy happens to produce good results, this is due to luck or inspiration. The true strategist depends on neither the one nor the other. He has a more reliable recipe for success: the combination of analytical method and mental elasticity that I call strategic thinking.

In my opinion, these two are complementary. For the strategic mind to work creatively, it needs the stimulus of a good, insightful analysis. In order to conduct a good analysis, it takes a strategic and inquisitive mind to come up with the right questions and phrase them as solution-oriented issues. Analyses done for the sake of vindicating one's own preconceived notions do not lead to creative solutions. Intuition or gut-feel alone does not ensure secure business plans. It takes a good balance between the two to come up with a successful strategy.

# 2
# Four Routes to Strategic Advantage

My concern in this book is not with strategic thinking in any abstract, general sense. Rather, I want to explore the way in which it can be used to develop more powerful business strategies. But before getting down to specifics, it is important to remind ourselves what business strategy is all about. Oddly enough, that is something that even full-time corporate planning staffs often fail to take fully into account.

What business strategy is all about—what distinguishes it from all other kinds of business planning—is, in a word, *competitive* advantage. Without competitors there would be no need for strategy, for the sole purpose of strategic planning is to enable the company to gain, as efficiently as possible, a sustainable edge over its competitors. Corporate strategy thus implies an attempt to alter a company's strength relative to that of its competitors in the most efficient way.

Of course, the condition or health of the business itself can be improved by reference to absolute criteria. For example, a company may seek to reduce the costs of its products by using value engineering or seek to improve its cash flow by shortening the collection periods for receivables. If successful, such efforts may bring added financial leeway through improved profitability. This in turn will widen the range of alternative strategies the company may choose to adopt vis-à-vis its competitors. These "operational" improvements can be regarded as a part of business strategy.

I believe, however, that it will make for clearer thinking if we reserve the term "strategy" for actions aimed directly at altering the strength of the enterprise relative to that of its competitors. We must distinguish these actions from actions aimed at achieving operational improvements, such as greater profitability, a more streamlined organization, more efficient management procedures, or improved training.

I make this distinction between relative and absolute strength because there is a great difference between the two with respect to the degree of urgency. Internal weaknesses or inefficiencies can usually be tolerated, at least for a time. By contrast, deterioration of a company's position relative to that of its competitors may endanger the very existence of the enterprise. In effect, it will allow the company's profitability to be controlled by its competitors, a situation in which sound management of the enterprise will no longer be possible.

Another reason for making this distinction is the fact that corporate strategy requires a specific type of thinking. When one is striving to achieve or maintain a position of relative superiority over a dangerous competitor, the mind functions very differently from the way it does when the object is to make internal improvements with reference to some absolute model. It is the difference between going into battle and going on a diet.

In the real world of business, "perfect" strategies are not called for. What counts, as we have seen, is not performance in absolute terms but performance relative to

**Business/Product Offered**

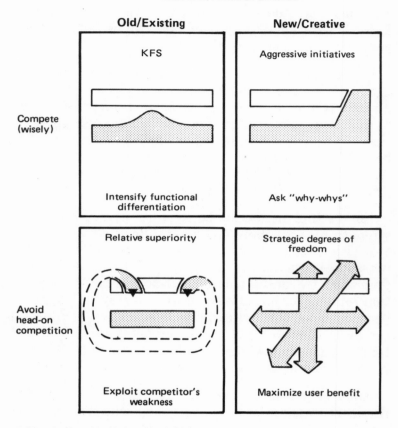

*Figure 2-1* Four basic strategies.

competitors. A good business strategy, then, is one by which a company can gain significant ground on its competitors at an acceptable cost to itself. Finding a way of doing this is the real task of the strategist.

How then does the strategist tackle this assignment? Basically, there are four ways of strengthening a company's position relative to that of its competitors (Figure 2-1).

1.  A company might readjust the allocation of the resources at management's disposal, with the object of strengthening certain of the company's capabilities in such a way as to increase its market share and profitability. If the management allocates the company's resources in exactly the same way that its competitors do, there will be no change in its relative position. The point in this method is to identify the key factors for success (KFS) in the industry or business concerned and then to inject a concentration of resources into a particular area where the company sees an opportunity to gain the most significant strategic advantage over its competitors. Even when the company has in effect no more management resources than its competitors in the same business or trade, it can often achieve resounding competitive success if it is effective in bringing those resources to bear on the one crucial point. I call this method business strategy based on KFS.

2.  Among companies competing within the same industry or business, there are cases in which even though a company enjoys no initial advantage over its competitors and the KFS struggle is being waged with equal vigor by all the companies concerned, a relative advantage can still be achieved by exploiting any difference in competitive conditions between the company and its rivals. Here the strategist's task is either to *(a)* make use of the technology, sales network profitability, and so on, of those of its products which are not competing directly with the target competitors, or *(b)* make use of any other differences in the composition of assets between the enterprise and its competitors. I call this method business strategy based on relative superiority.

3.  If the company's principal competitor is well established in a stagnant, slow-growth industry, that competitor may be hard to dislodge. Sometimes the only answer

is an unconventional strategy aimed at upsetting the key factors for success on which the competitor has built an advantage. To arrive at such a strategy, the starting point is to challenge the accepted assumptions governing the way of doing business in the industry or markets in question with a view to seeing whether it may be possible to change the rules of the game, upset the status quo, and thereby gain a novel and powerful competitive advantage. I call this approach business strategy based on aggressive initiatives.

4.   Even in cases of intense competition within the same industry or business, success in the competitive struggle can be achieved by the deployment of innovations. These innovations may involve the opening up of new markets or the development of new products. Both lines of action involve exploitation of the market by vigorous measures in particular areas untouched by competitors. I term this method business strategy based on strategic degrees of freedom.

In each of these four methods the principal concern is to avoid doing the same thing, on the same battleground, as the competition. To opt for a simple price war, for example, in which the competitors can easily follow suit, will not only harm the profitability of the industry as a whole but may very well strangle the strategist's own company in the bargain. Again, to cut product costs to the bone by exploiting every possibility for substitution of materials, relaxing quality standards, and the like, in the interest of increased profitability may well be self-defeating because in time it will weaken the product's consumer franchise and undermine the company's competitive position.

The aim of these four methods for strategic planning, therefore, is to attain a competitive situation in which your company can (1) gain a relative advantage through measures its competitors will find hard to follow, and (2) extend that advantage still further. The remarkable competitive performance of Japanese industry in recent years owes much to these approaches. In the next four chapters we shall be looking at each of them in turn to see how they have worked for individual Japanese companies.

My purpose will be to focus on the concepts that the strategists should consider, the thinking processes they should employ, and the kinds of conclusions and programs that should emerge. In themselves, the concepts of key factors for success, relative superiority, aggressive initiatives, and strategic freedom may seem simple and not worth making much ado about. But when these concepts are clothed in flesh and blood and used freely as tools in one's day-to-day business thinking, many a situation that might otherwise have loomed as a painful dilemma or hopeless predicament will present itself instead as a fascinating and stimulating challenge.

I will now explain each of these four routes to superior strategy in turn.

# 3
# Focusing on Key Factors

When resources of capital, people, and time are as scarce as they are today, it is vital to concentrate them on key functional or operating areas that are decisive for the success of your particular business. Merely allocating resources in the same way as your competitors will yield no competitive edge. If you can identify the areas which really hold the key to success in your industry and apply the right mix of resources to them, you may be able to put yourself into a position of real competitive superiority.

Identifying these key factors for success is not always easy. Basically, the strategist has two approaches at his disposal. The first is to dissect the market as imaginatively as possible to identify its key segments; the second is to discover what distinguishes winner companies from losers, and then to analyze the differences between them.

## Dissecting the market

Figure 3–1 shows how one Japanese shipbuilding company dissected its market into key segments as a preliminary to deciding where it would concentrate its major resources. Its products—tankers and cargo ships—are ranged down the left-hand axis. Note that this company doesn't regard tankers as a homogeneous product group; rather, it divides them into size categories. Similarly, its cargo ships are classified according to the degree of value added—namely, whether they are designed to carry high-, medium-, or low-grade cargoes, since high-grade cargo ships can be sold for twice as much per ton as low-grade vessels.

The different customers for each of these product lines, which are listed on the horizontal axis, have very different characteristics. For example, European first-class customers differ in importance and ordering patterns from European second-class customers, and Greek first-class shipowners behave differently from small Greek shipowners.

By segmenting the entire shipbuilding market in this way, the company was able to identify the wide range of product-market segments within it and also to recognize which segments were strategically important. Its next step was to develop product-market strategies for the crucial market segments and then assign responsibility for implementing segmentwide strategies. (In this case, the company appointed a regional manager with a sound knowledge of large bulk carriers to cover the Greek first-class shipowners.) Having developed a strategy and assigned responsibility for implementing it, the company then developed economic justifications—i.e., calculated the likely payoffs of the proposed strategies—for each segment, added all the resource requirements together, and finally revised the segment priorities in the light of available corporate resources.

Another Japanese company that dissected its market to good advantage was a manufacturer of forklift trucks. This company started from the realization that different segments of the forklift truck market have different product-performance requirements and that the needs of better than four out of five of its customers could be met by a vehicle costing 20 percent less to build than a machine designed to satisfy the entire market.

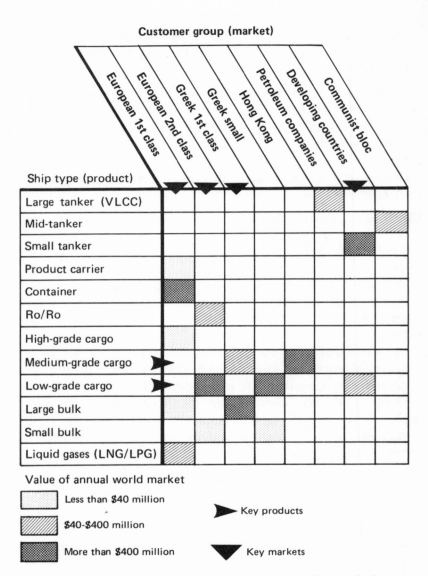

**Figure 3-1**  Shipbuilding product-market matrix (illustrative).

THE ART OF STRATEGIC THINKING

Having segmented its market and identified each segment's requirements, this company decided to concentrate on customers in the retailing and construction industries, leaving the more demanding segments (customers engaged in heavy-duty harbor and logging applications) to its competitors. This enabled it to introduce a lower-priced, value-engineered product line into a clearly defined target market segment, where it soon swept to a dominant position.

## Highlighting differences between winners and losers

Another and possibly more innovative approach to identifying the key factors for success is to discover what distinguishes winners from losers and why. Consider again the Japanese forklift truck industry. In terms of customer segmentation, it differs sharply from the truck industry. Only three customer industries account for 70 percent of all truck sales, whereas customers for forklift trucks are spread over a wide range of industries, among which the top three truck users account for no more than 30 percent of total forklift sales.

Now suppose a company that is making and successfully distributing trucks attempts to distribute forklift trucks as well. What will happen? Salespeople who are calling only on buyers in the truck industry's three main customer industries will find relatively few customers who are also customers for forklift trucks. They will miss the remaining 70 percent of the market, and their forklift truck sales consequently will be very small. On the other hand, a company with a good distribution network for forklift trucks will have little success if it tries to sell trucks in the same way. Although it will cover the entire truck market, it won't be able to give enough attention to the top three customer industries to win a dominant share.

It should not be surprising to find that companies with a large share of the forklift truck market have all adopted distribution networks designed exclusively for that purpose, whereas companies with distribution networks intended to serve both truck and forklift truck customers have achieved little success. Companies that fail to realize this basic fact are in danger of being swamped by competitors who know this key factor for success very well. In fact, one company, after recognizing this, saved itself by making the switch to a distribution network exclusively for forklift trucks.

The key factors for success of different industries, of course, lie in different functions, areas, distribution channels, and so on. Figure 3–2 shows how the key factors for success in gaining profit and gaining market share for different industries fall at different points along the stream of functional activities that begins with raw-materials sourcing and ends with customer service. For example, raw-materials sourcing is critical in the uranium industry, because low-quality ore requires much more complicated and costly processing. Since the market price for uranium does not vary among producers, the selection of the source of uranium is basically what determines each producer's profit.

In the soda industry, by contrast, production technology is the crucial factor. Since the mercury process is more than twice as efficient as the semipermeable membrane method of obtaining soda of similar quality, a company using the latter method will be unable to compete profitably, no matter what it does to reduce the extra cost. At the time it opts for the semipermeable membrane tech-

| Key factor or function . . . | Specimen industries | |
| --- | --- | --- |
| | ... to increase profit | ... to gain share |
| Raw materials sourcing | Uranium | Petroleum |
| Production facilities (economies of scale) | Shipbuilding, steelmaking | Shipbuilding, steelmaking |
| Design | Aircraft | Aircraft, Hi-Fi |
| Production technology | Soda, semiconductors | Semiconductors |
| Product range/variety | Department stores | Components |
| Application engineering/engineers | Minicomputers | LSI, microprocessors |
| Sales force (quality x quantity) | ECR | Automobiles |
| Distribution network | Beer | Films, home appliances |
| Servicing | Elevators | Commercial vehicles-e.g., taxis |

Upstream

Downstream

*Figure 3–2* How success factors vary by industry.

nology, therefore, a soda producer has already accepted a profit disadvantage vis-à-vis its competitors.

Exceptions, or singular points, always exist in the type

of model described above. Government regulations sometimes can alter these fundamentals—for example, by giving preferential treatment to less economically attractive technology in order to reduce mercury pollution.

Another interesting example of a key factor for success is found in the elevator industry. At least in Japan, nobody is patient enough to wait for hours to be rescued from a stuck elevator. Thus, once a company decides to enter this industry, it has automatically committed itself to establishing and maintaining an expensive servicing network. That, so to speak, is the fixed admission fee. Servicing cost is the crucial factor that determines the profitability of any elevator company.

## Identifying the KFS is not enough

When trying to search out the key factors for success in a particular industrial or business operation, the strategist needs to scrutinize the whole vertical chain of business systems involved, from raw materials to servicing after the products are sold to customers.

In the minds of the people engaged in the operation, all these factors normally crisscross in a complex patchwork, obscuring the individual stages of which the operation actually consists. To discern this overall pattern is the first task of the strategist.

That is not to say that corporate strategy must cover every stage of company operations, from raw materials through servicing, with equal thoroughness. Attempting to achieve decisive superiority all along the line would overstrain any pool of management resources, however large. Fortunately, control of one or two key stages will usually suffice to establish a position of competitive advantage.

Interestingly enough, the most effective shortcut to major success appears to be to jump quickly to the top rank by concentrating major resources early on a single strategically significant function, become really good and competitive at it, and then move to consolidate a lead in the other functions by using the profit structure that the early top status has made possible. All of today's industry leaders, without exception, began by bold deployment of strategies based on KFS.

Conversely, most businesses that have been left behind, although all their activities may have borne a surface resemblance to those of their more successful rivals, lost out either because they failed to perfect the function in which the all-important KFS were to be found, or because, having recognized the KFS, they lacked the thoroughness and persistence to exploit them fully.

Results do not automatically come just because one realizes where the KFS lie. The strategist must have the courage to gamble and accept the risks involved. This gamble—the strategic decision—is the narrow gate through which a company must pass if it is to win superiority in the demanding field of competitive business, particularly in head-on competition.

If you are fighting with a competitor who has equal qualifications, effective and persistent execution in critical functional areas may be the only differentiating factor. Toyota's persistence in rooting out waste from its organization and Hitachi's corporatewide management improvement (MI) activities are good examples of doing much better in areas everyone deals with anyway.

# 4
# Building on Relative Superiority

Although few product lines are identical, it should be possible for almost any company to compare its product with that of its competitors in order to identify unique product strengths on which it can build to develop market share. One way of doing this is to compare your product systematically with that of each competitor—physically tearing them down in the case of an assembled product—and analyze the differences in order to determine where you can achieve relative advantage either in price or in costs.

Suppose one component of your product is more expensive but better in quality than the one used by your competitors. Should you increase the retail price of the product to cover the extra cost of this expensive component? You will have to discuss this with your marketing staff. If they advise against a price hike, your salespeople should use this product advantage as a selling point (see figure on page 26).

An interesting example of relative superiority is found in the color film industry. Japan's amateur color film market is currently dominated by three companies, two of them Japanese: Fuji, which leads the market, and Sakura. For the past fifteen years, Fuji had been gaining market share, while Sakura—the market leader in the early 1950s with over half the market—had been losing share to both its competitors. Blind test results showed that the problem was not product quality. Rather, Sakura was handicapped by an unfortunate word association: its name in Japanese means "cherry blossom," suggesting a soft, blurry, pinkish image. The name Fuji, on the other hand, was naturally associated with the brilliant blue skies and white snows of Japan's sacred mountain. Sakura was gravely handicapped by its unfortunate image, but all its efforts to overcome the handicap through advertising were of no avail.

At length, Sakura turned to analyzing the market from structural, economic, and customer points of view to see whether it could uncover any opportunity to develop a positive competitive advantage. Here it came upon a clue.

What Sakura discovered was a growing cost-consciousness among film customers. Processors of exposed film reported that amateur photographers commonly left one or two frames unexposed in a 36-exposure roll but almost invariably tried to squeeze extra exposures from the 20-exposure rolls. Here was Sakura's opportunity. It decided to introduce a 24-exposure film at the same price as the competitors' 20-exposure film. Its marginal costs would be trivial, but its big competitors would face significant penalties in following suit. If they moved instead to lower the price of their 20-frame rolls, Sakura was prepared to do battle. Its aim was twofold. First, it would exploit the growing cost-mindedness of users. Second and more important, it would be drawing attention to the economic issue, where it had a relative advantage, and away from the image issue, where it could not win.

## The mechanism of relative superiority

One of the greatest obstacles confronting a company that tries to compete with the established giants, apart from the prodigious sales efforts such giants can deploy, is financial strength. If the situation should develop into a head-on price war, not many competitors would have the resources to hold out for long against one of the titans. It would, however, be even more difficult to compete with an established giant not in its primary business but in a business that it regards as secondary or has moved into for the sake of diversification. It is simple for the giant to shift the full weight of its resources to crush a would-be competitor in a peripheral area.

To understand in a little more detail the mechanism involved, let us imagine two manufacturers, Company A and Company B. Let us assume that plain-paper copiers are the area in which they are competing, although the same argument would hold for facsimile equipment or minicomputers.

Company A has such a dominant market share that it can determine its pricing policy from an almost monopolistic position. Although its cost structure suggests that costs per customer increase roughly in proportion to the total number of copies the customer makes monthly, its pricing is skewed. Small users are charged at below cost. This low charge constitutes a low admission fee for the new, inexperienced user, making it easier for the customer to install the appropriate machine.

Once the small user has installed Company A's product at a charge below cost, what follows? Company A has no particular love for the small user, since its account with that customer is in the red. But it will typically not stay in the red for long. What usually happens is that the small user gradually begins to exhibit the symptoms of copy addiction. The number of copies made mounts from one month to the next. Such is the universal human urge for possession and security that people in an office with a copier almost invariably get in the habit of telling their subordinates to copy this or that document and file it away just in case, even though the possibility of any future need for the document in question may be remote or nonexistent. Copiers stimulate demand for copies; hence Company A's price policy. So also with computers. When computer time was expensive, operators would check input meticulously, almost going to the length of working everything out on paper first. Now that the price has come down, the computer's time is often wasted. Operators no longer bother to check for faulty input but get the computer itself to indicate any error or let it go ahead with the calculations on the basis of mistaken input, not suspecting the presence of an error until the calculated output shows them an absurd result.

Copiers, then, constitute a business in which a low-admission-fee policy pays dividends. Such a policy means, however, that the prices charged to large users have to be relatively high, for there will be no overall profit if money is not earned in this small customer segment. Thus Company A's profit structure shows large earnings accruing from medium and large users, with a healthy overall profit emerging after taking into account the initial investment loss incurred with the smaller users.

Company A's pricing policy can be completely upset, however, if its diversified rival, Company B, enters the field. Let us suppose that Company B fixes its prices in strict relation to costs. Company B cannot win any customers among the small users because of Company A's tradition of low pricing in this segment. When it comes to the large users, however, Company B is competitive with Company A, and so it will be able to win a share of the market. Company A will then find that the proportion of unprofitable small users on its accounts is gradually rising, with a corresponding decline in the profitable larger users.

In consequence, Company A's profitability will begin to suffer, and Company A will find itself being forced into a very difficult position. Since copiers are Company A's main business, its only way of regaining lost market share in the large-user segment will be to adjust its pricing policy to something resembling that of Company B. Nevertheless, the effect of this change is likely to damage Company A severely because the company will be sacrificing the pillars of its profit structure.

The more bitterly each round of the struggle is fought, the deeper Company A will be plunged into trouble. If it cuts back on its small users, it is removing the foundation for any future recovery; when its small users develop into large users, they will switch to Company B. If Company A tries comprehensive cost-reduction measures and carries out a desperate price reduction, Company B will certainly engage in a price war. This will occur because Company B has other major sources of earnings besides its copier business and thus can stand a certain amount of losses on entering the copier market.

Thus for Company A the battleground will become a quagmire from which it is hard to escape, while Company B, with its strategy based on relative superiority, will slowly but surely win control of the entire market. Faced with this kind of unfair competition, Company A's strategy may be to fight in Company B's main business area in order to destroy Company B's major profit sources or at least demonstrate that it is prepared to retaliate.

Until recently, when international technical specifications to provide compatibility between different models of machines were agreed on, one of the key determinants of success in the facsimile business was the size of the machine population already installed. Customers wishing to install a facsimile machine would normally select the system that would allow transmission of information to as many potential recipients in the field as possible. Thus Company C, which might (and could afford to) treat the investment race as an initial investment aimed at securing a larger future share of the market, would naturally have an advantage over Company D, which might want the business to justify itself economically year in and year out.

I know a machinery company that developed a successful pricing strategy reflecting the fundamental difference between it and its major competitor in the economics of servicing. This company was able to make so much more money through after-sales service that it could afford to lower the price of its machines and thereby expand its share position. Its major competitor had long concentrated its efforts on sales of new machines, neglecting to make an adequate long-term investment in the field service force. Now, all of a sudden, it found itself having to fight on two fronts: depressed new machine prices and unprofitable service operations. Normally, it is hard to win this sort of fixed-cost game, based on a difference in profit structures between the two companies, against a competitor intent on exploiting an inherent relative advantage.

A position of relative superiority can be established in any number of areas. Detailed analysis of a product and its market may point out two or three possibilities for action. To formulate a corporate strategy that will be difficult for a competitor to imitate—and to ensure that the cost of imitation, if competitors do attempt it, will be heavy—the company either develops a completely new product or makes use of a position of relative superiority. The corporate strategist may not always be in a position to develop original new products, but rational and thorough analysis will often trigger an insightful strategy based on a position of relative superiority, using combinations of existing businesses and services.

# 5
# Pursuing Aggressive Initiatives

The strategist's weapons are strategic thinking, consistency, and coherence. With them, and relying on staff to provide the relevant knowledge or information, the strategist sets out to devise a method to clear away confusion and break the bottlenecks that have put the company into its current difficulties. No dramatic leap or stroke of genius is involved. The object of the quest is to come up with ideas or innovations that will introduce new life into the company's market situation, its resource allocation system, or anywhere else its existing practices have become rigid, thus enabling it to move forward in a specific direction.

The strategist's method is very simply to challenge the prevailing assumptions with a single question: Why? and to put the same question relentlessly to those responsible for the current way of doing things until they are sick of it. This way bottlenecks to fundamental improvement are identified, and major breakthroughs in achieving the objectives of the business become possible.

In a stalemated situation, it is very hard to bring about radical improvement through operational improvements, or doing more better. Such a stalemate usually comes about when both the cost and the effectiveness of striving for the key factors for success have reached the limit; the company's efforts to enhance the KFS no longer produce any discernible movement in market share or profitability, and the company finds itself drifting slowly in one direction over the years, usually deteriorating in the process. When this stage has been reached, the search for strategic measures becomes imperative. As far as operational improvement is concerned, the necessary premise is, as we saw in Chapter 3, a steady approach to the KFS. But to break out of a stalemate, the strategist has to take drastic steps.

The first step is to postulate that the company may have been led to the present stagnation by adhering to what had earlier constituted the key to success in respect to a given product or market. The KFS of Toyota and of Kirin Beer have been economies of scale in production and distribution, respectively. But if a weaker competitor wanted to effect a meaningful alteration in the balance of power in regard to a particular automotive vehicle or beer market, imitating the KFS that brought success to the established giants would lead only to its being ousted from the ring in a simple trial of brute strength. Hence the question the strategist should ask is, Have the KFS, in fact, remained unchanged?

What is called for, in other words, is a thoroughgoing challenge to the accepted common sense of the industry. The commonsense notions to be challenged may be located in such areas as actual production (method or process), distribution (sales and service network), or product planning. The more directly one is involved in each of these operations, the easier it becomes to overlook the commonsense issues that are there to be raised. For example:

¶ Why should fluorescent tubes be long and narrow?

¶ Why do we watch movies in the dark?

¶ Why should photographs have to go through the negative stage before being printed?

At first glance, such issues may sound unrealistic, a little like the intellectual games with which the philosophers of ancient Greece once amused themselves. But it is precisely by asking questions like these—challenges to the fundamental commonsense premises of business activity—that many outstandingly successful companies have managed to break out of seemingly hopeless competitive stalemates. Consider these examples:

The blankets produced by an electrical appliance manufacturer carried a warning: "Do not fold or lie on this blanket." One of the company's engineers wondered why no one had designed a blanket that was safe to sleep on while it was in operation. The engineer's questioning resulted in the production of an electric underblanket that was not only safe to sleep on while in operation but much more efficient. Being insulated by the other bedclothes, it wasted far less energy than conventional electric blankets, which dissipate half their heat directly into the air.

A camera manufacturer wondered why a camera couldn't have a built-in flash that would spare users the trouble of finding and fixing an attachment. To ask the question was to answer it. The company proceeded to design a 35mm camera with built-in flash. It was an enormous success, sweeping the Japanese medium-price lens-shutter market. Likewise, a camera company that questioned why exposed film so often came back without any pictures taken discovered that about 50 percent of Japanese women either couldn't load the film properly or were afraid to try. As a result it introduced an automatic film-loading mechanism that has eliminated the need to insert the end of the perforated film into a reel.

Mr. Taiichi Ohno of Toyota Motor Company wondered why it should be necessary to stockpile large quantities of components for production. As a result of his question, the company introduced a computer-based system that sends orders to its vendors, lists them in order of production, and gives the component suppliers—two or three weeks in advance—a production plan specifying type, quantity, delivery time, and order of delivery. A reminder, called *kanban,* is then circulated to suppliers so that they can deliver on time to meet the company's automotive assembly schedule. The conveyor belt acts as a buffer, and the suppliers hold the stocks of components they have produced right up to the time they are wanted on the main assembly line.

The key to this "just-in-time production" system is that the suppliers also use it to synchronize with final assembly production, thus eliminating work in process. And if anything happens to halt production on the main assembly line, the general manager is in a position to bring tremendous pressure on the supplier concerned to remedy the problem as swiftly as possible.

A commercial truck distributor noticed that his salespeople, like most others in the industry, were making most of their calls between 3 p.m. and 6 p.m. each day. He wondered whether orders peaked during that part of the afternoon, and he asked for a quick analysis. It showed that the period from 3 p.m. to 6 p.m. was precisely when the salespeople's success rate (the ratio of sales to calls) was at its lowest. Having established this point, management very sensibly relaxed its tight control on the salespeople's time, encouraging them to go straight to their territories instead of reporting to the office in the morning, and to take their free time in the afternoons. The end result: a significant share improvement for the company.

As these examples show, the best way to break out of a situation that has become excessively rigid over a long period of time is to shake things up a little by listing the most basic assumptions of the industry or trade one by one and asking whether they still hold or at least whether they are still vital to the continued existence of the business.

The results of this kind of change in the direction of strategic thinking can be spectacular. The basis of such an approach is always to confront what is taken for granted in an industry or business with the simple question, Why? If, instead of accepting the first answer, one demands the reason for *that* and persists in asking "Why?" four or five times in succession, one will certainly get to the guts of the issue, where fundamental bottlenecks and problems lie. All the great inventions of the past had their origin in this kind of inquisitive mind. To achieve similar quantum jumps in business competition, mortals like ourselves can take at least one leaf out of the great inventors' book and repeatedly and insistently pose the right kind of question.

# 6
# Exploiting Strategic Degrees of Freedom

The final route to superior competitive performance turns on the concept of the degrees of strategic freedom available to a company. This mode of thinking is particularly relevant for consumer goods companies and cost-conscious industrial goods manufacturers.

Normally, there is no possibility of improving performance in every operational area at once. That would be an option only if the resources at management's disposal—including time, energy, and attention—were unlimited. Because they are not, any realistic plan for strategic improvement has to be worked out within the constraints of the given finite resources. This means choosing a particular direction to pursue for success. Obviously, the choice of that direction is vitally important, and one of the most critical factors bearing on the choice is how much room for movement, or improvement, is available to the company in the direction being considered. If the KFS-based strategy discussed in Chapter 3 may be characterized as the way to find the key factor in a business operation, the concept of degrees of strategic freedom has to do with the amount of freedom for strategic moves in the area surrounding a particular key factor.

Suppose, for example, that the company is competing in a high-technology field and that therefore the crucial factor for competitive success is in the technological area.

Until it is clear in which direction of technological innovation an opportunity for strategic moves will present itself, there will be no prospect of improvement. Take the case of an automaker and suppose that this direction has been identified. In order to raise the market share of its cars, the company has to build more safety into them. Looking at the problem from the angle of the car body, areas for constructive change toward more safety would fall into various categories: improvements in visibility, instrumentation, ventilation system, fatigue-free seats, braking system, suspension system, energy-absorbing body structure, etc.

## Selecting the critical axes

Although the theoretical possibilities for improvements affecting traffic safety are innumerable—including, for example, better roads and signals—not all of them are available to the car manufacturer. In practice, the strategic moves that a given car manufacturer can adopt are limited. When cost-effectiveness and possible retaliatory moves by competitors are taken into account, it will be clear that a strategy to pursue improvement along a few selected axes is much more likely to produce the desired results.

The term "strategic degrees of freedom" (SDF), as I use it, designates the axes along which such a strategy can realistically be worked out. In the case of cars, for example, it can be said that there are two degrees: improvements in the industrial engineering aspects (exemplified by the first four items mentioned above) and improvements in the mechanical system.

The object of assessing the degree of strategic freedom is simply to avoid the waste of time and money that is bound to ensue if management fails to determine in advance the best direction for improvement. We must first try to grasp the whole picture and then ask in which direction or directions our resources should be concentrated to give us the best possible chance of capitalizing most effectively on the key factors.

A crucial element in the SDF concept is that of the *objective function,* the value or variable we wish to maximize. A manufacturer's objective function, for example, might well be profit; more specifically, perhaps, earnings of 15 percent on the stockholders' investment, at least over the next five years. An individual executive's objective function might be achievement, or to make a million dollars before age 40. A customer's objective function could be interpreted simply as what he or she is looking for from the product. In any case the objective function is critically influenced by a number of independent factors, or degrees of strategic freedom. The SDF concept is therefore both the starting point and driving force of this kind of strategic thinking.

### Cases in point

Consider the example of a coffee-making business. Suppose we have determined through market research that the objective function of our target customers is superior taste. What can we do to deliver that? What are the variables that fundamentally determine the taste of a cup of coffee?

When we think about it, there are quite a number: kind and quality of the beans, type of roast, fineness of grind, elapsed time between grinding and brewing, water hardness, water temperature, mode of contact between water (or steam) and ground coffee, temperature at which the brewed coffee is maintained, elapsed time between brewing and drinking, and so on.

These are just a few of the variables that can change the taste of a cup of coffee. Some of them, being outside the manufacturer's control, don't qualify as degrees of freedom. Others, such as hardness of water, are conceivably within the manufacturer's power to affect (for example, by incorporating a regenerable filter in the machine) but are conventionally regarded as out of bounds. This means that we are not fully utilizing the degrees of freedom available to enhance the user's objective function, i.e., taste in this case. Instead of continuing to think in terms of the conventional alternatives—Should we make a percolator or a filter pot? Would the users go for glass or aluminum?—we ought to look for unexploited degrees of freedom and ask what possibilities they may harbor. Whether A is better than B, or C is better than D, may be the obvious issues—but it is only by going outside of them and looking at K, Q, and Z that we will ever hit on a source of real competitive differentiation. Figures 6–1 to 6–3 illustrate how these same concepts might apply to the design of an innovative product in another consumer goods category, microwave ovens.

Or take another example, although a little extreme, in the automobile business. What is the user's objective function? Basically, we can say that it is to move individually and freely from one place to another, perhaps in the shortest time and at the least cost or with the least fatigue. Existing motor vehicles certainly do not meet these objectives, because they are constrained by availability and conditions of the road. An ideal vehicle would be able to move as the crow flies. Yet despite the limitations of their product, automakers today are not investing in the development of any helicopterlike vehicles that

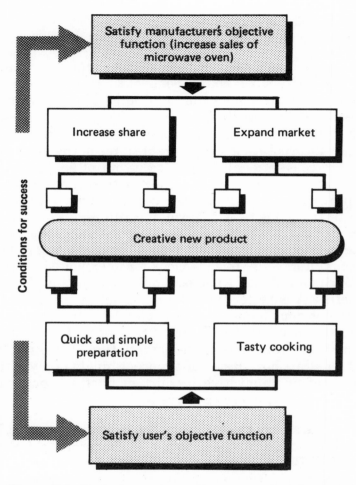

**Figure 6–1** Designing an innovative new product for success.

could eventually free people from the constraints of the earth's surface. They seem to believe that they are still locked in combat with the railways, and hence they are quite often found lobbying for investing more tax dollars in highways than in public transportation.

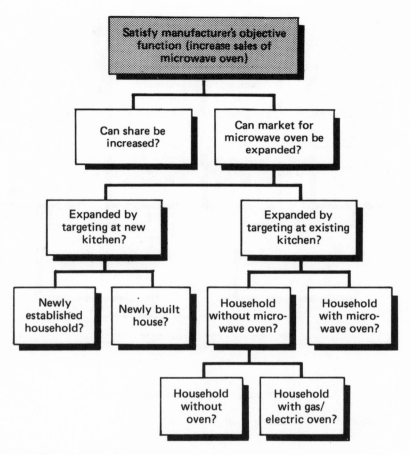

**Figure 6-2** The manufacturer's objective function.

Likewise, wristwatches may not be the ultimate answer to the objective of knowing the time. I no longer need to wear one in downtown Tokyo because there are so many clocks everywhere. Is a bed the best device to sleep on? Is a compressor-driven air-conditioner the best device to cool a room—or to make the occupants feel cool

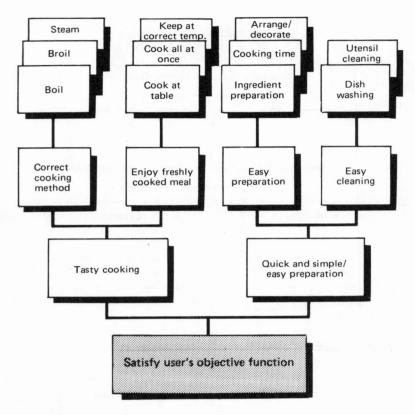

*Figure 6–3* The user's objective function.

(their objective function)? The answers are not so obvious as they might seem. In formulating a product-market strategy, it will often pay handsomely to question whether our product line is fully meeting the user's true objective or whether other and better ways of satisfying the same objective are available or even thinkable.

The amateur photography business offers another interesting example. The consumer's objective function is to get dependably excellent pictures at a reasonable cost. To maximize this objective function—i.e., to increase user benefit—the manufacturer has a variety of options. As illustrated in Figure 6–4, there are probably at least seven kinds of options (shown in the chart as axes) that offer scope for significant improvement. The first axis is the film, which will affect the quality (grain, color tone, etc.) of the finished photograph. The second axis, which is decisive for the quality of the image, is the lens and the associated optical factors. The third is the mechanism, in particular the shutter. The fourth is the light source; the fifth and sixth, the quality of the printing paper and the conditions of laboratory development. Finally, there is the skill of the camera user. By forcing various ideas along each axis, it is possible to develop a series of distinctive strategies. Along the film axis, for instance, the number of exposures could be changed; the tone of the film could be differentiated for natural indoor exposures, portraits, and so on; graininess could be reduced further; the speed of the film could be increased; or, in an extreme case, a "posi-posi" film could be developed that would permit color prints to be made directly, eliminating the need for a negative.

## Fighting on multiple fronts

Since we are not at the moment dealing with an actual business situation, let us assume for simplicity's sake that three axes—film, accessories, and lens—have finally been selected as the axes for strategic technological innovation (Figure 6–5). The number three has no special significance other than as a useful reminder that we are not competing in a unidimensional business. Hostile competitive moves can come at us from at least three different directions, and we should therefore have our defenses

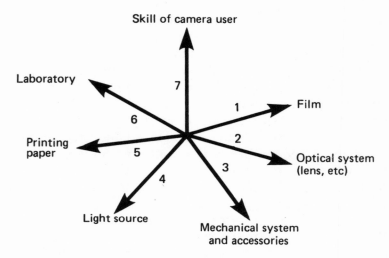

**Figure 6–4** Degrees of strategic freedom for improving quality of finished photographs.

ready for all three of them. By the same token, though, the number three reminds us that there is little possibility of attacks by competitors coming from all directions at once. The choice of three strategic axes amounts to a message from the general staff to the battlefield commander: "If our defenses are sound on these three sides, battles can be fought and won."

Along each axis of strategic freedom, a series of points can typically be located, corresponding to the principal moves that companies engaging in this business can take in the attempt to secure competitive advantage.

As Figure 6–5 shows, the degrees of freedom for strategic moves on the film axis include number of exposures, color tone, speed, and resolving power. These areas are not selected at random but are derived by analysis aimed at identifying those factors which theoretically exert the

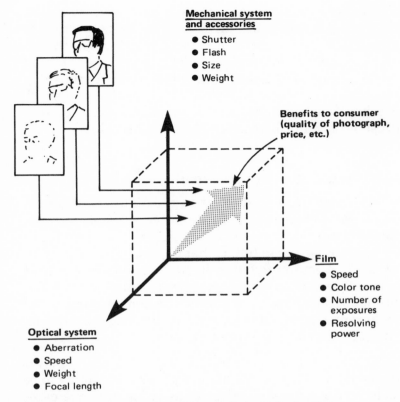

**Mechanical system and accessories**

- Shutter
- Flash
- Size
- Weight

**Benefits to consumer (quality of photograph, price, etc.)**

**Film**

- Speed
- Color tone
- Number of exposures
- Resolving power

**Optical system**

- Aberration
- Speed
- Weight
- Focal length

*Figure 6–5*  Three selected degrees of strategic freedom.

largest influence on the finished photograph. The four points in question represent the areas in which improvement is most practicable, i.e., where a given expenditure of resources seems most likely to produce significant technological results.

Having come up in this way with a certain number of points along the various axes of strategic freedom, we can make an estimate of the cost and effect of carrying out an improvement at each point. The effect may be expressed in terms of either market share or profitability. In the initial stages, this effect will increase in proportion to expenditure up to a certain point, beyond which the return on investment will level off or decline. This, of course, is the well-known phenomenon of diminishing returns. In some cases there will be an incubation period. In other words, no return will appear until a certain threshold level of investment has been reached.

## Exploiting degrees of freedom

In any event, we will do well to calculate the probable investment-versus-return curve for each point, or node, along the axes of strategic freedom being considered. Our calculations will soon tell us that depending on the different product and production facility development efforts involved, each of our strategic moves would have a different incubation period, a different cost-benefit impact, and a different point of diminishing returns against the investment required to implement it.

Our next step is to try to forecast which of the moves represented by the points along each axis are likely to be made by competitors, and in what order. In some cases there will be different competitors along each axis. Bearing in mind the respective cost-effectiveness of these moves for each of our competitors, the damage they may inflict on us, and the time it will take us to launch our new model or models, we can then determine an appropriate sequence for our strategic moves. They should add up to a strategy that will maximize user benefits at minimum cost by using the available degrees of strategic freedom to the best possible advantage.

For example, we might decide to introduce reduced-weight accessories, add 24-exposure film, change the tone, or design a camera with built-in flash, meanwhile working to develop a film that will appeal to both cost-conscious customers and to those wanting a built-in flash. Next, the company could adopt an automatic range finder to further improve the exposure, modify the lens, increase the speed of the film, introduce an electronic shutter to reduce the mechanical vibration of the camera system, and so on.

In the meantime, a competitor may have decided to introduce a faster color film. In this case, the first manufacturer could move immediately to the electronic shutter to improve the picture and reduce the failure rate; then the manufacturer could go on to develop a posi-posi film, thereby shifting the battleground away from negative film altogether. Clearly, to coordinate these ideas and actions demands the discipline of a single, coherent, carefully worked out strategy.

In conventional, "reciprocal," head-on competition, the rules of the game are simple. If your competitor cuts the price, you cut yours; if the competitor introduces a cheap product, so do you. Such tactics may work, but never very well or for very long. Ultimately, they may lead to a fatal erosion of profitability. In contrast, the method I propose —first determining the degrees of strategic freedom and then making a thorough study of the possibilities along each axis on which freedom has been shown to exist—will often produce an abundance of profitable strategic ideas within a very short period of time.

## Segmenting by user objective

Strategically, it makes sense to segment the market according to user objectives, for the basic reason that one can then develop a *differentiated* set of strategies to satisfy a distinctive group of users who have the same objective. For example, television manufacturers know that color balance is more important than sharp definition to the user with a large living room, while the reverse is true of the user whose viewing must be done in cramped quarters.

The user's objective function, however, can change with time or with advances in product technology and cost. Wristwatches used to be differentiated by accuracy, which reflected the cost of manufacture and therefore price. But now, in the wake of mass-produced large-scale integrated (LSI) chips and frequency oscillators, accuracy is no longer a source of differentiation. Accordingly, successful watchmakers have rather quickly shifted their emphasis. Elegance and high fashion have become the main sources of differentiation in satisfying user objectives. Whether this strategy will work is not yet clear; if it turns out that most watch buyers are satisfied to have accuracy without the frills, the end result could be a significant loss in the value added of this industry.

Again, in the component stereo industry, the user's objective function, and hence the manufacturer's main source of product differentiation, used to be performance as measured by power output, signal-to-noise ratio, transient response, and the like. But now that almost all the surviving manufacturers can deliver similar performance characteristics, the major source of product differentiation is no longer the quality of sound reproduction but the physical size of the equipment, i.e., miniaturization of individual components so that they will not take up so much space in the user's living room. Massive physical size, once associated with high performance and higher price tags, no longer offers prestige value for the customer, at least in Europe and Japan. Thus, when the company's investments aimed at better satisfying users' current objectives reach a point of diminishing returns, the strategic thinker will explore other user values and search for strategic degrees of freedom to satisfy them by means of technology, service, and the like. Recognizing in advance such changes in the users' objective function and stretching one's mind to find the SDF by which the new objectives can be satisfied is one way to become a pioneer in the new-business game.

# 7
# The Secret of Strategic Vision

A broad ribbon of concrete winds its way through the beautiful forests of northern New York State. It passes through Rochester, home of Kodak, and links Schenectady, where General Electric has plant locations and a research and development (R&D) laboratory, to Buffalo, where Dunlop Tire and Rubber has its U.S. headquarters. Driving along the Thruway, one often sees the bodies of deer lying dead on the road.

Even for an automobile, let alone its occupants, a high-speed collision with an animal as big as a deer is a serious matter. A former classmate of mine had his car badly damaged when a deer ran out of the woods, evidently intending to cross the road, but then stopped in its tracks as if it had momentarily lost its bearings. In the next instant, catching sight of my friend's oncoming car, the animal lowered its head and charged the vehicle head-on. The sudden apparition of the car must have paralyzed the deer's judgment, causing it perversely to rush in the fatal direction when it could have escaped with seconds to spare.

People can experience a similar kind of mental paralysis. I can remember driving once at very high speed along the Pennsylvania Turnpike and experiencing a curious hallucination. The broad three-lane highway seemed to contract to the width of a single lane, which itself converged to a point not very far ahead. At the same time, my own visual field narrowed sharply. Despite a kind of subconscious urge to widen it, I found myself able to see only straight ahead, as though some external force had seized me. In such extreme conditions, a human being may be just as likely as a deer to make a fatal blunder.

## Strategic tunnel vision

Business executives are no exception. The more severe the pressure and the more urgently a broader view is needed, the more dangerously their mental vision seems to narrow down. This is especially likely to be true of a businessman who is obsessed with the idea of winning and sees everything in terms of success or failure. Such an executive may be almost unable to perceive that there is any room for intelligent choice among various courses of action. Yet if that executive would try changing the objective from success at all costs to avoiding the worst, he would be sure to find a great many possible choices opening up.

In Japan as in the West, it is not unheard of for major companies to fail outright. But I know of no such company that could not have changed direction before it was too late. In each case I have observed, management, at a certain point in time, simply lost sight of the range of alternatives that were still open and rushed with ever-narrowing mental vision to their own destruction.

## The "all or nothing" fallacy

No business in the real world operates according to the clear-cut, on-off, black-or-white principle of the binary system. In its responses to environmental change as well as the effects it is able to achieve through its own strategic initiatives, every company is subject to the analog principle exhibited in all organic processes: the principle of infinite variability. Total success may be unattainable, yet problems can be brought under control, obstacles can be overcome, and the worst can be avoided. Although the battles management has to fight are real, there is always a chance for competitive revival as long as the company is solvent.

For companies that are already within sight of success or well on the way to it, my task as a professional consultant is to help management set an ideal goal to aim at and to work out concrete measures for achieving it. For companies in decline and headed for catastrophe, I almost always try to imagine the worst possible case and then work out ways and means of avoiding it.

Strategic thinking in business must break out of the limited scope of vision that entraps deer on the highway. It must be backed by the daily use of imagination and by constant training in logical thought processes. Success must be summoned; it will not come unbidden and unplanned. Top management and its corporate planners cannot sensibly base their day-to-day work on blind optimism and apply strategic thinking only when confronted by unexpected obstacles. They must develop the habit of thinking strategically, and they must do it as a matter of course. Ideally, they should approach it with real enthusiasm as a stimulating mental exercise.

To become an effective strategist requires constant practice in strategic thinking. It is a daily discipline, not a resource that can be left dormant in normal times and tapped at will in an emergency.

There is no such thing as a line of ready-made packaged strategies waiting to be picked off the supermarket shelf. The drafting of a strategy is simply the logical extension of one's usual thinking processes. It is a matter of a long-term philosophy, not of short-term expedient thinking. In a very real sense, it represents the expression of an attitude to life. But like every creative activity, the art of strategic thinking is practiced most successfully when certain operating principles are kept in mind and certain pitfalls are consciously avoided.

## Flexible thinking

Because he understands the full range of alternatives that lie before him and constantly weighs the costs and benefits of each one, the true strategic thinker can respond flexibly to the inevitable changes in the situation that confronts the company. And it is that flexibility which, in turn, increases the chances of success.

Considering alternatives requires us to pose "what if" questions. In other words: If the situation were such-and-such, what would be our best course of action? But when it comes to thinking, we are really very lazy. Perhaps the reason may have something to do with a lack of self-confidence in regard to the thinking process itself. In any case, we don't like to push our thinking far enough or take the "what if" questions very seriously.

In some companies, managers have long since abandoned any pretense of bold thinking. They have become simply salary takers, devoid of any sense of entrepreneurship or competitive urgency—and these are precisely the qualities needed for success in a decisive conflict. The thinking process required of the marketing manager who is working out a particular product-market strategy is no less demanding than that required of the military staff officer who is drawing up a strategic plan for an infantry engagement. In fact, the two have several parallels. The first relates to the importance of pragmatism in pursuit of the objective.

**Perils of perfectionism.** In competing for market share, there is no sense trying to draw up a "perfect" strategy. The denominator of the market share is the sum of one's own sales and those of the competitors; to beat the competition, a strategy that is even marginally superior will suffice.

What *is* vital is timing. The most brilliant strategy will be useless if it fails to take account of the ever-changing trends of the market. The key to victory, then, lies in developing a market strategy that will give you an edge— even a slight edge—on the competition and then putting it into effect at exactly the right moment.

In very much the same way, the role of the staff officer in a battle is to discover (or forecast as rationally as possible) the enemy's strength and operational plans and, based on that discovery or forecast, to devise a strategy that will put his side one step ahead of the enemy. Victory will go to the side that has a single soldier left on the battlefield. Thus, especially when our forces are outnumbered, it is essential to get them into action with no waste of time or motion. If a commander fails to confront the situation boldly and postpones vital decisions for fear of casualties, he is likely to find his battalions cut away from under him.

For the military strategist, then, the key is to judge how far the quest for the ideal strategy should be carried and to determine the point at which perfectionism becomes a liability. If the strategist is determined to eliminate even the most minute blemish in his strategy, his staff officers will need perfect information and unlimited time to work it out. The commander who stands atop a hill near the battleground, putting the last touches on a flawless scheme for victory while his troops are being driven from their positions, is as much of an incompetent as the officer who loses a battle through flagrant miscalculation.

It should be clear now, I hope, why I have chosen to compare business strategy with military science. There is important common ground between the task of the military strategist on the one hand and the key strategic activities of middle and top management on the other: grasping the state of the market, objectively assessing the strengths and weaknesses of one's business, changing direction with flexibility when required, and calculating the amount of profit or loss likely to result from each management action. Both the business strategist and the military planner are prone to be trapped by perfectionism.

**Keeping details in perspective.** A related vice is timidity. All too many people in responsible management positions seem unable to make well-timed decisions on their own. Some may have climbed the management ladder by relying on other people's judgments. Some may lack the requisite basic information or the ability to analyze properly the meaning of the information they do receive. But even the competent, the well informed, and the analytically minded may be subject to a perfectionist obsession with detail, leading to a compulsion to qualify, a fear of asserting that such and such is definitely the case. Behind this fear lies intellectual timidity—a distrust of all definitive answers, a hopeless feeling that problems are too complex and many-sided to yield to clear-cut solutions. This, of course, is a classic instance of self-fulfilling defeatism.

There is a simple remedy available to managers who are inclined to worry too much about details in the process of reaching an overall judgment that may have only a 90 percent probability of being correct. They should write down each point of uncertainty, estimate the probability of a positive or negative outcome in each case, and assess the probable impact on the overall result if each decision should end in a negative outcome. If it turns out, as it often will, that a negative outcome from each of the unresolved uncertainties won't affect the overall result significantly, the manager can and should brush the uncertainties aside and proceed boldly with the overall judgment.

Having once chosen their direction, many successful Japanese entrepreneurs, such as Konosuke Matsushita and Soichiro Honda, obstinately persisted with execution of their plans regardless of minor shifts in circumstances. In contrast, many large, institutionally run companies tend to insist on getting everything exactly right when it comes to working out the details of a plan. As a result, they allow business opportunities to pass them by. Sometimes, indeed, their efforts are directed at perfecting the details of a strategic plan that is directionally completely wrong.

Fine-tuning the details when only a change in the basic course of action can ensure success makes about as much sense as rearranging the deck chairs on the *Titanic*. For example, efforts to improve the accuracy of mechanical watches are pointless today because electronic oscillators have made accuracy a nonissue. A real strategic issue here would be the choice between developing the lowest-cost pin-lever watch with tolerable accuracy, for sale in

Third World markets where even the cheapest watch is still a costly luxury, and moving into electronic watches and developing programs to ensure high value added (e.g., through image or design) against competitors with equal accuracy.


## Focus on key factors

Paradoxically, the manager who has succeeded in freeing himself from perfectionism in the sense just described will need to practice it in another sense. In one area, and one area only, obsessive thoroughness—thoroughness to the point of perfectionism—does have its place. In the pursuit of the key factors, the strategic thinker cannot afford to be anything less than a perfectionist.

In any business situation, a handful of the myriad factors present will basically determine the outcome, and strategy will be successful if these factors can be controlled or applied skillfully. We have called these the key factors for success.

Banking, for example, appears to the lay person as a fearfully complicated business, requiring immense sophistication to grasp. In a sense this is true. Yet the key factor in the banking world is nothing more abstruse than discovering how to amass money cheaply and lend it at as high a price as possible—finding the right "mix" so that the cost of capital to the bank is kept to a minimum and the return kept to a maximum.

In shipbuilding and steelmaking, once a certain production technology is chosen, economies of scale in manufacturing are the key to supremacy. In the beer industry, to take another example, the key factor is again economies of scale—but economies of scale in distribution, not manufacturing. Or take ice cream. There the key factors are two: the ability to control seasonal variations and the ability to ensure economic refrigeration capacity throughout the distribution process.

A strategic thinker never allows himself to lose sight of the key factors in the business or operation for which he is responsible. With that constant awareness, he will shape his strategy—a strategy not for total war on all fronts but for a limited war on the fronts defined by the key factors for success. It is perfectionist pursuit of these key factors—nothing more or less—that brings in the profits. In other words, it is this focus on key factors that gives the major direction or orientation to the operation we call strategic thinking.

### Probing for KFS

As a consultant faced with an unfamiliar business or industry, I make a point of first asking the specialists in the business, "What is the secret of success in this industry?" Needless to say, I seldom get an immediate answer, and so I pursue the inquiry by asking other questions from a variety of angles in order to establish as quickly as possible some reasonable hypotheses as to key factors for success. In the course of these interviews it usually becomes quite obvious what analyses will be required in order to prove or disprove these hypotheses. By first identifying the probable key factors for success and then screening them by proof or disproof, it is often possible for the strategist to penetrate very quickly to the core of a problem.

Traveling in the United States last year, I found myself on one occasion sitting in a plane next to a director of one of the biggest lumber companies in the country. Thinking

I might learn something useful in the course of the five-hour flight, I asked him, "What are the key factors for success in the lumber industry?" To my surprise, his reply was immediate: "Owning large forests and maximizing the yield from them."

The first of those key factors is a relatively simple matter: the purchase of forest land. But his second point required further explanation. Accordingly, my next question was: "What variable or variables do you control in order to maximize the yield from a given tract?"

He replied: "The rate of tree growth is the key variable. As a rule, two factors promote growth: the amount of sunshine and the amount of water. Our company doesn't have many forests with enough of both. In Arizona and Utah, for example, we get more than enough sunshine but too little water, and so tree growth is very low. Now, if we could give the trees in those states enough water, they'd be ready in less than fifteen years instead of the thirty it takes now. The most important project we have in hand at the moment is aimed at finding out how to do this."

Impressed that this director knew how to work out a key factor strategy for his business, I offered my own contribution: "Then under the opposite conditions, where there is plenty of water but too little sunshine—for example, around the lower reaches of the Columbia River—the key factors should be fertilizers to speed up the growth and the choice of tree varieties that don't need so much sunshine."

Having established in a few minutes the general framework of what we were going to talk about, I spent the rest of the long flight very profitably hearing from him in detail how each of these factors was being applied.

## Challenging the constraints

When you are working out your strategy, if you start by thinking of all the things that cannot be done and then merely ask yourself what possibilities are left, you will almost certainly be unable to break out of your existing situation. This is the point that worries me most in my conversations with executives. When a problem crops up in a given area, I try to find out first how the managers responsible for that area see the problem and then what proposals they have in mind for solving it. Their attitude almost always turns out to be some variation on: "The way things are, there's not much *we* can do. Top management at the corporate level doesn't really understand what's going on. . . . The quality of our people isn't what it used to be. . . . We're really hamstrung by government regulations. . . . It's a losing battle; they (the competition) have just got too much clout with the distributors, and there's no way we can fight that."

As an outsider, I can take a third-party view, and so I ask: "Tell me, what precisely are the limiting factors that have convinced you nothing can be done?" In this way, we can start to define the constraints or conditions.

My next question: "What alternatives would be open to you *if all these constraints were removed?*" If they think they are blocked from taking action by such factors as personnel, funds, or corporate image, I ask them to imagine that they have been given a free hand in all these matters and to outline what kind of solution to their current problems they would envision in that case. After a pause, they will say hesitantly, "Well, the most desirable solution would be. . . ." or "Ideally. . . ." Then I know I have set them on the right track.

If the strategic thinker can generate an awareness of what an ideal state of affairs might be, even if it seems unattainable at present, constraints that have loomed as absolute can be seen rather differently—as potentially surmountable obstacles to the attainment of the ideal solution. Strategic thinking can then be concentrated on ways of removing these obstacles.

When there is no common recognition within an organization of the ideal goal and the obstacles to its attainment, managers' energies are all aimed in different directions, and progress toward remedying the problem is all but impossible. Once such a common recognition is achieved, however, all concerned can apply their joint energies to removing the obstacles to a solution. Thus, by directly challenging the constraints, the strategic thinker usually finds that in reality they are far less formidable than they had appeared.

## Strategic schizophrenia

A corporation I know decided, for reasons too complicated to explain here, to split off manufacturing and sales as two separate companies. Twice a year, joint planning conferences were held to determine the selling prices and the numbers of each product model to be produced in the next six months. In time the two companies came to regard each other as enemies, and the semiannual conference turned into an arena of mistrust and conflict. The people involved began to think the problem was insoluble.

But a closer look suggested something quite different. Amazingly, the two sides lacked a common data base at the planning stage. Each was producing its own cost estimates and market forecasts, and since they started every discussion on the basis of their own one-sided figures, a satisfactory solution was impossible from the outset.

Since the two companies were nothing but two functions of a normal integrated company, it was obvious that the solution had to lie in some form of recentralization. In the event, a new directorship was set up spanning both companies, with the two planning staffs integrated under it in a single group that was made responsible for producing a single, unified plan.

## A question of attitude

It is far from my intention to stress individual solutions to particular problems. Problems vary as much as fingerprints, and so do the solutions. History, environment, and previous policies all exert subtle influences to make each problem unique. In the business world there is really no such thing as a ready-made answer to a particular strategic problem.

However—and this is my point—a change in the attitude of those who must confront the problem can work wonders. The secret lies in making people think, from the very start, What can we do? instead of What can't we do? and then striving doggedly to strip away one by one the constraints that have turned the possible into the seemingly impossible.

Corporate performance is the result of combining planning and execution. It resembles a boat race. No matter how hard each crew member rows, if the coxswain doesn't choose the right direction, the crew can never hope to win. Conversely, even if the coxswain is a perfect navigator, you cannot win the race unless the rowers strive hard in unison.

# Part 2
# Building Successful
# Strategies

# 8
# The Strategic Triangle

In the construction of any business strategy, three main players must be taken into account: the corporation itself, the customer, and the competition. Each of these "strategic three C's" is a living entity with its own interests and objectives. We shall call them, collectively, the "strategic triangle."

Seen in the context of the strategic triangle, the job of the strategist is to achieve superior performance, relative to competition, in the key factors for success of the business. At the same time, the strategist must be sure that his strategy properly matches the strengths of the corporation with the needs of a clearly defined market. Positive matching of the needs and objectives of the two parties involved is required for a lasting good relationship; without it, the corporation's long-term viability may be at stake.

But such matching is relative. If the competition is able to offer a better match, the corporation will be at a disadvantage over time. If the corporation's approach to the customer is identical to that of the competition, the customer will be unable to distinguish between their respective offerings. The result could be a price war, which may bring short-term benefits to the customer but will hurt the corporation as well as its competitors. A successful strategy is one that ensures a better or stronger matching of corporate strengths to customer needs than is provided by competitors.

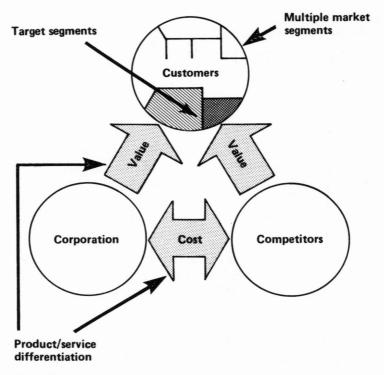

*Figure 8–1* The strategic three C's.

In terms of these three key players, strategy is defined as the way in which a corporation endeavors to differentiate itself positively from its competitors, using its relative corporate strengths to better satisfy customer needs (Figure 8–1).

## Strategic planning units

For a large company made up of a number of different businesses selling to different customer groups, there is clearly more than one strategic triangle to be dealt with and more than one strategy to be developed. The question is, How many? At what level in the organization does it make sense to try to develop a strategy?

To develop and implement an effective strategy, a business unit needs to have full freedom of operation vis-à-vis each of the three key players. With respect to *customers,* it must be able to address the total market, not just its sections. If the strategic planning unit is defined too narrowly—i.e., placed too low in the organization—it may lack the authority to take a total market perspective. This will be a handicap if the competitors' perspective takes in the entire needs of the customer, including some that cannot be detected through the limited lens of a business unit. For example, if a customer is looking for integrated electronic components, the supplier who offers only a specialized switch will be at a disadvantage.

In order to be able to respond with maximum freedom to the total needs of the customer, the strategic planning unit (SPU) needs, in terms of the *corporation* itself, to encompass all the critical functions. These functions might range all the way from procurement, design and engineering, manufacturing, and sales and marketing to distribution and service. This is not to say that the SPU may not share certain resources—e.g., R&D—with other units. Rather, it means that a good business unit strategy must address all the functional aspects of customer needs and competition. A conventional organizational unit may not have every key function reporting to it, but in strategic planning one needs to explore every possibility of utilizing the corporation's relative strengths to achieve differentiation from the competitor. Such differentiation comes only from differences in functional strengths, singly or in combination.

Unable to achieve competitive differentiation by strengthening its distribution and service network, a Japanese manufacturer of air-conditioning equipment decided to do so by developing a line of sturdy, highly reliable, but expensive home air-conditioners. Being an engineering-oriented company, it could do this very well. What it couldn't do, it turned out, was sell the product.

In fact, it failed to achieve a share of even 1 percent, and for a reason that had never entered management's head. Distributors, the real decision makers when it comes to brand selection, rejected the new line completely. Why? The units were too heavy to be lifted by an ordinary two-person installation crew. Instead of thinking through the strategic implications of all the key functions, this manufacturer had resorted to its favorite solution—engineering—prematurely.

Existing functional strengths can, of course, often be successfully exploited to gain the desired differentiation. Another company, a maker of plain-paper copiers, was handicapped by a relatively weak servicing network compared with that of its dominant competitor. Recognizing its functional weakness, this company decided to compensate by exploiting its strengths: engineering, manufacturing efficiency, and quality control. It developed a line of machines that had just two advantages over the competitor's offerings: they were relatively service-free and slightly cheaper. This combination enabled the company to increase its market share rather quickly.

## Broad perspective needed

In addition to surveying all the corporation's critical functions, the strategist must be able to look at *competition* in its totality, including such critical strategic elements as the competitor's R&D capabilities, shared resources in procurement, manufacturing, sales and service, or other sources of profit (including all the other businesses in which the competitor may be engaged). He must also be able to put himself mentally in the place of a strategic planner in the rival company and thus ferret out the key perceptions and assumptions on which the competitor's strategy is based.

Faced with a major worldwide shipbuilding crisis, Mitsubishi Heavy Industries has been able gradually to shift its permanently employed excess shipbuilding labor to its other businesses and subsidiaries, such as automobiles, chemical plants, power plants, and its other metal-forging and fabrication operations. Because its competitors lacked Mitsubishi's flexibility, their shipbuilding became extremely uncompetitive and unprofitable.

Strategic planning units, then, are best established at a level where they can freely address (1) all key segments of customer groups that are similar in needs and objectives, (2) all key functions of the corporation so that they can deploy whatever functional expertise is needed to establish a positive differentiation from the competition in the eyes of the customer, and (3) all key aspects of the competitor (see Figure 8–2) so that the corporation can seize an advantage when opportunity offers—and conversely, so that the competitors will not be able to catch the corporation off balance by exploiting unsuspected sources of strength.

## Definitional problems

Strategic planning units should not be defined so narrowly that they lack the required degree of freedom vis-à-vis the strategic three C's. For example, a strategy for farm tractor engines would be ineffective because the strategic unit is at too low a level in the organization to (1) consider product applications and customer groups other than farmers, or (2) cope with competitors manufacturing en-

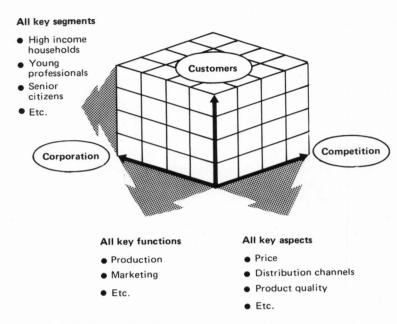

**All key segments**
- High income households
- Young professionals
- Senior citizens
- Etc.

Customers

Corporation

Competition

**All key functions**
- Production
- Marketing
- Etc.

**All key aspects**
- Price
- Distribution channels
- Product quality
- Etc.

*Figure 8-2* Essential dimensions of a strategic planning unit.

gines for marine, truck, and/or construction equipment applications, or even with general-application original equipment manufacturer (OEM) specialists, who might enter the farm tractor market at almost any time with products having a totally different set of boundary conditions. A better choice for this strategic business unit might be small diesel engines, because such units would potentially have a broad enough perspective and adequate strategic degrees of freedom.

By the same token, a strategic planning unit that is too broadly defined cannot develop a really effective strategy. For example, a strategy for medical care would embrace equipment, service, hospitals, education, self-discipline, and even social welfare. Each of the three key players—the strategic three C's—might consist of dozens of totally different elements with different objectives and functions, making the interaction matrix a nightmare of complexity. Such a strategy would have to be expressed in the most general terms or developed in very great depth at enormous effort, to permit a reasonable understanding of the strategic thrust for the corporation. A more sensible strategy could be constructed for an intermediate unit making related kinds of equipment, e.g., blood analyzers, tomographic scanners, and back-room electronic data processing (EDP) systems. The reason is simply that at this level, where a fairly consistent group of customers and competitors with similar needs and wants appears, functional differentiation—be it in terms of technology or distribution—becomes possible.

We see other examples of wrongly defined strategic business units in the likes of a "strategy" for hospital supply logistics, a "strategic plan" for the XYZ Company's purchasing department, or an Agriculture Ministry's "strategy" for its irrigation program. The problems addressed in these examples lack one or more critical dimensions of strategy. When no competition exists, there is no need to strategize; the need is rather to think about how to make operational improvements in the service provided to the customers or recipients. Another weakness in such strategies is the lack of sufficient degrees of freedom in the planning unit. The scope of the strategy is restricted to one or two functional departments, which may be unable to respond to the total needs of the customer, let alone to a comprehensive attack by competitors.

## Testing the decision

Business unit definition always leaves room for dispute. Halfway into the process of strategy development, therefore, when the basic parameters of the three key players have become clear, it is a good idea to reassess the legitimacy of the unit originally chosen by asking three key questions:

1.  Are customer wants well defined and understood by the industry, and is the market segmented so that differences in those wants are treated differently?

2.  Is the business unit equipped to respond functionally to the basic wants and needs of customers in the defined segments?

3.  Do competitors have different sets of operating conditions that could give them a relative advantage over the business unit in question?

If the answers give reason to doubt the business unit's ability to compete effectively in the market, the unit should be redefined to better meet customer needs and competitive threats.

In the next three chapters we will be surveying the broad categories of strategy, with each chapter focusing on a particular point of the strategic triangle: the customer and the market environment, the corporation itself, and the competition.

Nothing is more self-contradictory than to talk about "creative" strategic thinking and, in the next breath, to give codified recipes for developing strategies of various sorts. Rather than that, my purpose will be to show that an initial focus on any one of the three key players must eventually lead back to its strategic tie-in with the others. Accordingly, the shrewd strategist will always try to view the strategic three C's in perspective and try to influence the dynamics of the relationships among them so as to expand the corporation's relative advantage.

# 9
# Customer-Based
# Strategies

In a free economy, no given market remains homogeneous, since each customer group will tend to want a slightly different service or product. But the corporation cannot reach out to all customers with equal effectiveness; it must distinguish the easily accessible customer groups from the hard-to-reach ones. Moreover, the competitor's abilities to respond to customer needs and to cover different customer groups will differ from those of the corporation. To establish a strategic edge over its competition, therefore, the corporation will have to segment the market—it must identify one or more subsets of customers within the total market and concentrate its efforts on meeting their needs. Fine structure within the customer group offers the opportunity to establish this kind of differentiation (Figure 9-1).

## Segmenting by objectives

There are two basic modes of market segmentation. The first is segmentation by objectives, i.e., in terms of the different ways different customers use the product. Take coffee, for example. Some people drink it to wake up or keep alert, while others view coffee as a way to relax or socialize (coffee breaks). Preparation methods, taste preferences, the amount consumed at a time, and even the type of cup used for serving may all differ among different

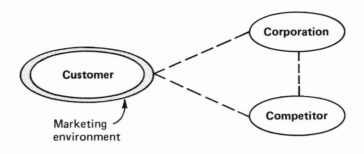

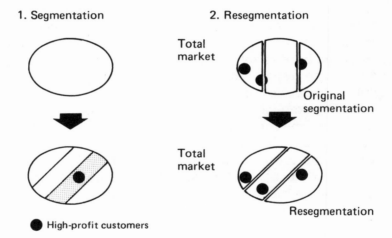

● High-profit customers

*Figure 9–1* Achieving competitive differentiation through customer segmentation.

customer groups. Although both groups may be handled by the "coffee" business unit, the segment that uses coffee recreationally can be grouped with the home entertainment or leisure-time market.

In market segmentation the effort is to understand whether different subgroups are in fact pursuing objectives that are different enough to warrant the corporation's (or the competitor's) offering differentiated services and products. Obvious differences in age, race, profession, region, family size, and so forth, may be the basis of segmentation, but usually these constitute convenient statistical classes rather than strategic segments. Differences per se are not good enough unless each segment has differentiable objectives that can be reflected in the way the corporation approaches the market.

This is why it is so important to understand the fine shades of customer wants. Purchasers' decision-making behavior often reflects the degree of utility, quality, or luxury the particular customer groups may demand at given price levels. The price-quality relationship is important to the sophisticated customer, while price alone may be more important to other customers. Since price increases tend to depress demand in most markets, the very size of the customer group is itself a function of the pricing decision.

The value that a customer perceives in a product or service he or she may decide to buy can range from intangibles such as glamor, ego satisfaction, luxury, or brand image to tangible attributes such as performance, durability, running cost, comfort, resale value, payment terms, availability of spare parts, or convenience of sales and service outlets. Since the value the customer perceives in the product will differ according to his or her needs and wants, a careful analysis of these will often lead to strategically effective segmentation.

## Segmenting by customer coverage

Another mode of segmenting the market may arise from the corporation's own circumstances. Even when there is a large group or subgroup of customers who have similar wants and needs, the corporation's ability to serve them all may be constrained by limited resources, by gaps in market coverage relative to the competition, or by the cost of serving a fragmented market at a price acceptable to the customer, who, if the price is too high, can always go without the product or resort to an alternative: a radio instead of a TV set, a lead pencil instead of a fountain pen, a bus instead of a taxi.

This type of strategic segmentation normally emerges from a trade-off study of marketing costs versus market coverage. Marketing costs—which may include the costs of promotion to establish brand awareness, sales activities, servicing network, inventories to provide adequate delivery, physical distribution, and commissions and margin to motivate dealers and distributors—are typically dictated by the desired speed and depth of penetration into the target customer group. There appears always to be a point of diminishing returns in the cost-versus-coverage relationship. The corporation's task, therefore, is to optimize its range of market coverage, be it geographical or channel, so that its cost of marketing will be advantageous relative to the competition.

As shown in Figure 9–2, sophisticated companies often have a clear matrix framework for strategic segmentation, distinguishing the cut by customer objectives (Type I) from the cut by their own market-coverage capability (Type II). The crucial task here is to ensure that the corporation can positively differentiate its products and/or services from those of the competition in each of the chosen segments (corresponding to the shaded boxes marked ● in the matrix).

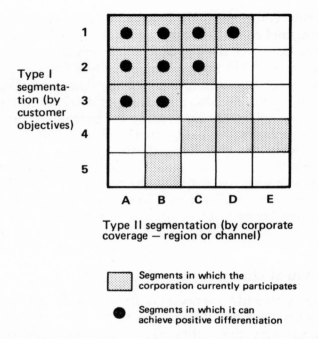

Type I
segmentation (by
customer
objectives)

Type II segmentation (by corporate
coverage — region or channel)

Segments in which the
corporation currently participates

Segments in which it can
achieve positive differentiation

*Figure 9-2* Matrix framework for strategic segmentation.

## Resegmenting the market

In a fiercely competitive market, the corporation and its
head-on competitors are likely to be dissecting the market in similar ways. Over an extended period of time,
therefore, the effectiveness of a given initial strategic segmentation will tend to decline. In such a situation, it
often pays to pick a small group of key customers and
reexamine what it is that they are *really* looking for. A
maker of facsimile equipment, accustomed to classifying
customers by machine performance—i.e., high-speed (1
minute) and low-speed (4 to 6 minutes)—decided to investigate why larger corporations typically had few if any
machines and showed little interest in purchasing the

available equipment. He learned that the typical large account had coast-to-coast coverage, with many regional outlets. But since the fast and slow machines were incompatible and could not be linked, it was impractical for them to set up national networks. The manufacturer then decided to develop a medium-speed (2-minute transmission) machine, resegmenting the market according to the customers' need to establish local, regional, or national networks. By providing these customer groups with slow, medium, and slow-medium modular plus fast trunkline equipment, respectively, the company could afford to drop the most difficult customers, who required many interfaces between slow and fast machines.

## Structural changes

Market segments are perpetually in flux. Environmental forces are constantly changing customers' likes and dislikes, altering the utility of product lines, and shifting purchase priorities. Among other forces, trends in the sociopolitical environment, new government regulations, and replacement threats coming from other types of products and services will inevitably cause shifts from time to time in the relative positions of each of the strategic three C's. Whenever these shifts occur, they present the corporation with fresh opportunities and threats.

We have already seen that there are two types of segmentation: the first by customer wants, the second by market coverage. Correspondingly, market segments may undergo two possible types of structural change: one owing to the changes in user objectives over time, the other owing to the changes (either geographic or demographic) in the distribution of the user mix. Structural changes normally oblige the corporation to shift its resources either across functions or across product-market segments (e.g., from Northeast to South Central).

## Changing applications

If the user's objectives are changing over time, the corporation will be obliged at some point to think about offering a different product or service. Since the late 1960s, for example, new economic forces have changed the cost-benefit objectives of many car owners from high-speed travel and prestige to convenience, economy, and utility. This led to the introduction by Honda, Suzuki, Daihatsu, and some European car companies of small town cars for customers interested primarily in driving relatively short distances for shopping and other errands in congested urban areas. In the same way, costly jet fares were justified only because time had become the scarcest resource of all for most businesspeople.

Again, Mitsubishi Electric Company's domestic space heater, which draws in the outside air to provide for gas combustion and vents the carbon dioxide out of doors, has been a phenomenal success in Japan because people have become increasingly health- and environment-conscious. A decade ago, when people were buying heaters simply to keep warm, the space heater would have been uncompetitive because its operating cost was marginally higher than that of the kerosene stove. Likewise, sales of battery-powered forklift trucks are growing in Japan, despite the low power and complicated maintenance requirements of the product, simply because operators are getting fed up with the noise, vibration, and exhaust gases produced by diesel- and gasoline-powered models.

By influencing the user's objectives, fundamental forces like these create a multitude of replacement opportunities. Instead of regarding this phenomenon as a mere change in product mix—e.g., from engine-powered to battery-powered lift trucks—we should try to understand its fundamental causes. Only then will we be able to anticipate its impact: which segments are likely to change, how much further the shift is likely to go, and what factors will influence the rate of change. Strategically, the corporation needs to establish a better position than the competition in emerging market segments. By offering differentiated products that will have a stronger appeal to the new breed of customer than to the old, it can take advantage of the forces at work in ways most likely to enable it to grow faster, and more profitably, than its competitors.

## Changes in customer mix

The second category of market segment change occurs where the forces at work are altering the distribution of the user mix over time by influencing demography, distribution channels, customer size, and so on. This kind of change calls for shifting the allocation of corporate resources and/or changing the absolute level of resources committed in the business. Unless resources are appropriately reallocated in the light of whatever structural changes have occurred, the growth of a market segment in which the company is relatively weak can lead to a severe loss in total market share.

For example, a truck manufacturer discovered that single-truck owners were increasing relative to large-fleet owners. This company was very strong in the corporate account segment, with a fully dedicated sales force. However, it was weak in the fragmented single-truck-owners segment, where the competitors were successfully relying on dealers to push their products. Although percentagewise this manufacturer's share of both corporate and private account segments remained virtually constant, its overall share of the market was declining, largely because of the relative growth of a segment in which it was badly underrepresented (Figure 9–3).

To correct the situation, management could either increase its direct sales force to enable it to cover the fragmented private segment effectively or bolster its distribution by locating dealers whose sales and distribution resources could be shared with complementary or competitive corporations. In this instance, the manufacturer could afford to choose the first course. It expanded its sales force by 20 percent, using it exclusively to chase after the single-truck owners, and within a year and a half it had increased its share of this growing segment by more than 5 percentage points.

Similar changes are taking place in office equipment (e.g., plain-paper copiers), retail electronics (e.g., electronic cash registers), and construction equipment. In fact, very few companies lose market share in head-on competition. In my experience, in the majority of instances a corporation loses market share because of structural changes, i.e., the faster growth of its weak segment compared with its strong segment.

## Keeping tabs on trends

Structural changes are usually slow, incremental processes, imperceptible from year to year to those inside the business. A definite trend is likely to emerge only over a prolonged time span, say five to ten years. It is therefore critical in strategic planning to analyze changes in the relative importance of market segments over a rather extended period of time.

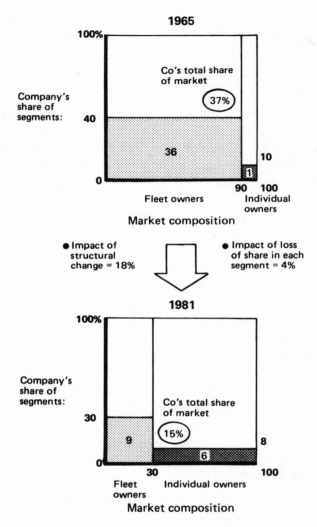

**Figure 9-3**  Impact of structural changes on a truck maker's total market.

If significant changes have occurred, the first step is to analyze the forces at work and extrapolate them just far enough into the future to ensure that the company is "reading" the environment slightly ahead of its competition. If government action or an economic discontinuity such as the energy crisis causes a precipitate change in the boundary conditions in the market, management will have to ask whether the impact of the change calls for a change in strategy and/or timely action to preempt any new business opportunities that may have been opened up by the forces at work.

Customer-based strategies are the basis of all strategy. Unless the company objectively views its customers' intrinsic needs as they change over time, its competitors will some day challenge the status quo. There is no doubt, therefore, that a corporation's foremost concern ought to be the interest of its customers rather than that of its stockholders and other parties. In the long run, the corporation that is genuinely interested in its customers is the one that will be interesting to investors.

In a free, competitive economic world, there will be no stability in a corporation's performance if it allows its attention to be diverted from the basic business mission of serving its customers. If it consistently succeeds in serving customers more effectively than its competitors, profit will follow.

Too many corporations today lose sight of this, even to the point of forgetting what business they are in. Like Japan's prewar *zaibatsu* holding companies or the loosely coupled U.S. conglomerates of recent decades, they tend to enter businesses more or less indiscriminately and run them very much alike. Few such companies ever manage to build a business and sustain a profitable leadership position.

# 10
# Corporate-Based Strategies

Unlike the customer-based strategies we have just been considering, corporate-based strategies are functional. Their aim is to maximize the corporation's strengths relative to the competition in the functional areas that are critical to success in the industry.

## Identifying key functions

Once the customer's needs and objectives are analyzed and understood, the corporation's strategy would normally be to meet them in the most cost-effective way. But strategies are not framed in a vacuum. The competition will soon discover what the corporation is doing and follow suit. If this happens, the only way the corporation can profitably survive the head-on competition is to be much stronger in one or more key functions. These differ not only from industry to industry but also with respect to the strategic objective (share or profit) sought. As noted in Chapter 3, the profitability of the uranium business depends heavily on sourcing. Since the yellow cakes are sold at about the same price worldwide, access to rich ore deposits can give a company a critical advantage in extraction and refinery costs, overshadowing any difference in downstream strategies.

Again, in a commodity component market such as

switches, timers, and relays, both market share and profitability are heavily influenced by product range. Ordinarily, an engineer who is designing circuitry reaches for the thickest catalog with the broadest product selection. In this industry, therefore, the manufacturer with a wide selection can collect share points from the competitors even though his sales force may be relatively meager. This double advantage over companies in the opposite situation (i.e., those with fewer selections and hence lower sales effectiveness) explains why company performance in this kind of business tends to be polarized. It is easy to say that the weaker company needs to strengthen the sales force, but given its low volume and high fixed costs, that could carry a severe profit penalty. The key functions in this business, then, are design engineering, and manufacturing. The corporation will need to develop many product lines with fewer people than the competition and/or have superior plant layouts and labor skills in order to produce many different product types and sizes without proportionately augmenting its fixed costs. These are the basic functional strengths required to compete in an industry in which the key factor for success is breadth of product range.

Maintaining a positive differential in key functional strengths is vital to retaining an advantage in profit performance and market share. A company that analyzes customers and competitors but fails to strengthen the functions that are critical for success in the industry is like a staff-dominated military with a weak combat force.

### Selectivity and sequencing

In order to win, however, the corporation does not need to have a clear lead in every function from sourcing to servicing. If it can gain a decisive edge in one key func-

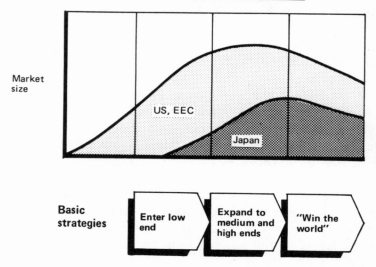

**Figure 10–1** Japanese "win" strategies.

tion, it will eventually be able to pull ahead of the competition in other functions that may now be no better than mediocre. But the process does not work in reverse. A chief executive who invests in improving all functions may achieve the desired operational improvement, yet the corporation can still end up a loser because its performance in a single key function is still much inferior to that of the competition.

The secret of many Japanese corporations' success is their skill in sequencing the improvement of functional competence (Figure 10–1). In the 1950s and early 1960s many of them made heavy investments of both money and talented people in manufacturing engineering. Their production technology, together with the advantage in labor cost they enjoyed at that time, constituted their principal source of strength. At this stage, their invest-

BUILDING SUCCESSFUL STRATEGIES

## Basic strategy: Enter low end

**Strategic emphases**

- Market analysis
- Production technology
- Southeast Asia
  (experimentally, US)
- Trading firms

**Representative products**

- Computers
- Gas turbines
- Compressors
- Construction equipment
- Large-scale integrated
  circuits
- Color film

## Basic strategy: Expand to medium and high ends

**Strategic emphases**

- Economies of scale
- World market
- "High class" image
  orientation
- OEM or own brands

**Representative products**

- Turbines/generators
- Plain paper copiers
- Pianos
- Automobiles
- Telecommunication
  equipment

## Basic strategy: "Win the world"

**Strategic emphases**

- Global brands (more
  than two companies)
- Non-price competitiveness
- Overseas production
- Continued innovation
  (prolong life cycle)

**Representative products**

- Cameras
- Stereo equipment
- Tape decks
- Personal calculators
- Motorcycles
- Watches
- Steel

**Past the peak (shift to NICs)**

- Radios
- TV
- Textiles
- Shipbuilding
- Plywood

**Create new market**

- VLSR
- VTR

ments in research and development and overseas marketing were minor; for these they relied on imported technology and trading firms, respectively. Later they shifted their emphasis to quality control and product design capabilities. Today they are very active in basic research and direct marketing. At each phase they have been able to generate the money to reinvest in improving the next generation of functional strengths.

In some industries, the key functions are extremely dynamic. For example, the key to survival in the semiconductor industry is the ability to shift emphasis rapidly from one area of functional expertise to another. Constant investment in R&D facilities, manufacturing engineering, productivity improvement, and quality control would be too costly. What needs to be strengthened is not each of these functions per se but rather the corporation's ability to shift the resources, both capital and human, required in each functional area in step with the rapid change in key functions that takes place in the course of a given product's life cycle. Figure 10–2 graphically illustrates this process in the case of a particular type of integrated circuit made by one Japanese manufacturer.

### Functional strategies

The corporation's functional strategies should be clearly distinguished from operational improvements. The latter are aimed at "doing better"; they rest on the implicit assumption that cost reduction is good across the board (i.e., for any key cost center, regardless of strategic implications). The former require a thorough understanding of customers (their needs and objectives and their geographical and demographical distribution) and of competitors (their behavior and relative strengths and weaknesses).

BUILDING SUCCESSFUL STRATEGIES

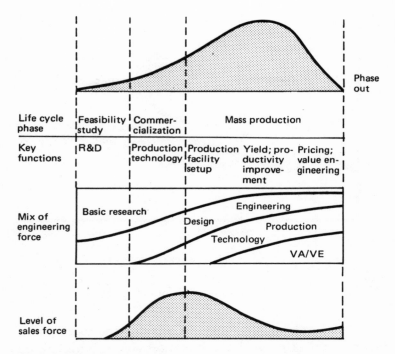

**Figure 10–2** Shifting human resources as key functions change along a product life cycle.

Functional strategies must also be distinguished from operational programs designed to improve particular organizational units such as engineering, purchasing, or marketing. Their object is not to solve the operating problems of a particular department but to strengthen the specific functional performance required to succeed in a given industry. To be sure, responsibility for this function may currently be assigned to a particular organizational unit, and in such a case functional strategy may fall under an existing department. But this is by no means always the case; in some companies a specific function may neither be assigned to any particular department nor performed collectively.

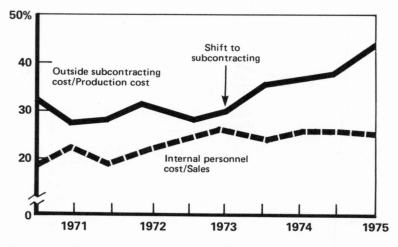

Source: Fujitsu annual reports and Yukashoken Hokokusho (Japanese equivalent of 10 K reports)

**Figure 10–3** Fujitsu's strategic shift in make-buy policy.

**A case of make or buy.** Consider the example of a large corporation with a labor-intensive assembly operation that is confronted by a rapidly increasing labor rate and growing fringe-benefit costs. In such a situation, the "make-buy" decision may well become the key function. Few companies, however, treat make-buy decision making as a key function to be perfected. Mostly it is left to the procurement agent and/or to a manufacturing planner who is worried about unused production capacity.

Figure 10–3 shows the results of a change in make-buy policy made by a large Japanese computer company, Fujitsu. Although the company never publicly announced any such policy shift, it is clear from this analysis (based on published data) that Fujitsu's change of course in 1973 reflected a critical strategic decision, in response to rising wage costs, to subcontract a major share of its assembly operations. Its competitors may not have been able to shift production so rapidly to subcontractors and vendors, and the resulting difference in cost structure and/or in the company's ability to cope with demand fluctuations could have significant strategic implications.

**Casio versus the competition.** Another example is Casio, a manufacturer of watches and pocket calculators. Most of its competitors are organized around the traditional functions of engineering, manufacturing, and marketing and have gone in heavily for vertical integration, for example, through ownership of dedicated integrated circuitry (IC) production facilities. Casio, in contrast, even today remains basically an engineering, marketing, and assembly company, with very little investment in production facilities and sales channels. Its strength is flexibility. Recognizing its competitors' inability to introduce new products rapidly, Casio has adopted a strategy of accelerating and shortening product life cycles (Figure 10–4). No sooner had its 2mm-thick, card-size calculator been introduced than Casio started rapidly bringing down the price, thus discouraging its competitors from following with a similar product. Within a few months, Casio introduced another model, which emits musical notes as the numerical keys are touched.

In Casio's case, the functional strategy is to integrate design and development into marketing so that consumers' desires are analyzed by those closest to the market and quickly converted into engineering blueprints. Because Casio has this function so well developed, it can afford to make its new products obsolete quickly. Its competitors, all organized vertically on the assumption of a one- or two-year life cycle for this type of product, are at a severe disadvantage. As a result, psychological warfare developed between departments in some of these competi-

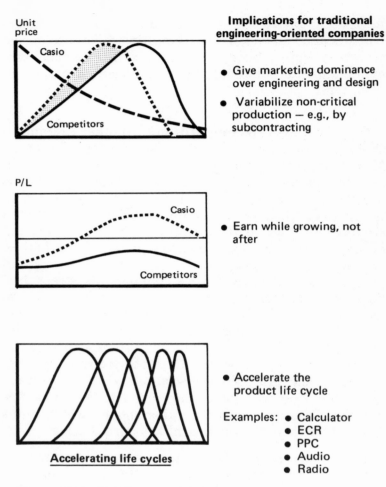

**Implications for traditional engineering-oriented companies**

- Give marketing dominance over engineering and design
- Variabilize non-critical production — e.g., by subcontracting

- Earn while growing, not after

- Accelerate the product life cycle

Examples:
- Calculator
- ECR
- PPC
- Audio
- Radio

*Figure 10-4* Casio's competitive strategy.

tor companies. Engineering, for instance, can no longer trust what marketing says, and vice versa.

When it runs out of new ideas and its customers get fed up with the accelerated life cycles, Casio will have a major problem, for it has little differentiable expertise in the traditional functions of production, logistics, and sales. The company's current success, however, may indeed enable it to gradually strengthen these functions sufficiently before the time bomb explodes.

Casio also alerts us to the danger of blind faith in the traditional product-life-cycle theory that the best strategy is always to invest to gain share during the growth phase. Instead, the new lesson in these industries is that a company needs to earn as it grows—a difficult balancing act but potentially a highly rewarding one, as Casio's example shows.

These examples of functional strategies underline a key point. Once an organizational unit has been defined, it may be too late to think about a functional strategy. The best approach to developing such a strategy is to ignore organizational boundaries to begin with and instead to develop a detailed understanding of customers and competitors in order to identify the functions that are critical to success.

Having done this, we can turn to the question of whether the existing organizational units, individually or collectively, are performing these key functions better than they are performed by the competition, and if not, what needs to be done to provide a competitive edge. In some cases, the final solution may entail a basic organizational change. In others, it may suffice to assign a few added responsibilities to existing departments or to push for significant improvements in certain management processes.

## Optimizing functional performance

A corporate function usually represents a fixed cost. The engineering department of a semiconductor house, for example, may account for as much as 20 percent of total corporate costs. Such a department behaves exactly like a facility; there is a certain threshold in the size of the engineering staff above which continuous innovation is possible but below which nothing seems to go right.

The sales function is also a fixed cost, although a company could certainly choose to make it variable by depending heavily on distributors and the like. Once properly in place, it becomes a stable corporate strength. A "subthreshold" sales force, on the other hand, could be a constant source of problems. The optimum size of these functions—or, putting it another way, the optimum fixed cost of performing a given function—is determined by the other key players in the strategic triangle: the customer and the competition.

A fragmented market usually requires a dense distribution network to provide reasonably uniform service to all the customers. In a situation where one competitor is dominant, however, the level of service to the customer can be lowered significantly. Kodak, by far the biggest U.S. film manufacturer, provides a certain standard developing and printing service for mail-order customers. Other customers can drop off the film in person and pick up the finished prints several days later. To process film, Kodak has centralized its labs in six strategically located centers in the United States, which, from the point of view of a manufacturer intent on reaping economies of scale, provides a great advantage. But from the customer's point of view, two days to a week is still a long time to wait for prints. Thus Kodak's focus on establishing economies of scale in laboratory operations invited a challenge from Polaroid with its concept of instant pictures.

By contrast, in Japan three film companies compete

fiercely for share and have had to continuously upgrade their service to customers. As a result, there are 300 processing laboratories today in a country no bigger in landmass than the state of California, and the proportion of total films processed on a seven-hour pickup basis is rapidly approaching 30 percent. Despite massive promotional campaigns, instant photography of either the Kodak or the Polaroid variety is hardly a factor in Japan, except in certain highly specialized professional applications. One hears a lot about the heated competition in instant film, but once some company seriously tackles the fundamental issue of what users really want—namely, to get their pictures back in a hurry—competition in instant photography in the U.S. could cool off dramatically. More than half the time, having instant prints doesn't matter to users of instant cameras.

Again, a film developing and printing network is a fixed cost. No company can afford to improve or invest in all the key functions of its operations indefinitely; it must make a strategic choice among the alternative functional areas for investment. And yet the dilemma remains. A company can achieve a lower fixed-cost position if its throughput is substantially higher, but to achieve higher throughput normally entails a higher fixed cost of operation, be it in the sales force or the production facility.

**Improving cost-effectiveness**

Thus, the other main object of functional strategies is to design and deliver *cost-effective* functions. This can be done in three basic ways. The first is by reducing costs (through overhead value analysis, zero-based budgeting, or whatever) much more effectively than the competition.

The second method is simply to exercise greater selectivity in terms of orders accepted, products offered, or functions to be performed. Functional costs typically build up in proportion to the sheer quantity of work involved (number of bids and number of workers) rather than to sales dollars per se. Greater selectivity means cherry-picking the high-impact operations so that as others are eliminated, functional costs will drop faster than sales revenues.

One Japanese machinery manufacturer with only a tiny market share was offering a product selection almost as varied as that of the industry leader, who had 45 percent of the market. None of the smaller manufacturer's product lines was profitable. Its problem, however, was not in the design of individual product lines but in the high overheads resulting from disproportionately high development and distribution costs allocated across the board. This sort of situation becomes a vicious cycle unless top management fundamentally alters its policy and shifts from a jack-of-all-trades approach to the market to a very selective segment-by-segment strategy. Once this manufacturer was persuaded to prune its product line and concentrate in segments where other market coverage was not essential to success, such as fleet owners, its situation improved dramatically.

The third method of reducing functional cost is to share a certain key function among the corporation's other businesses or even with other companies. Although it can result in complications and psychological warfare, resource sharing can also provide an opportunity to obtain the same functional performance at much lower cost, thus gaining a critical advantage over competitors who do not have similar business arrangements.

Typical examples of shared resources are the pooled sales force and account manager concepts seen in sales organizations. In a business where customer relationships or the frequency and density of calls are more important than specific product knowledge, these are effective means of sharing a sales force among different product-business units. If the competitor's sales force is organized around individual business units, he will find it very hard to respond in a way that will satisfy the two conflicting requirements of high market coverage and low sales cost.

Experience indicates that there are many situations in which sharing resources in one or more basic subfunctions of marketing can be advantageous. This is true of service, financing, promotion, and advertising as well as physical distribution; the one clear exception seems to be product planning. In fact, according to a Heidrick & Struggles survey of marketing executives, about half of U.S. manufacturers have centralized promotion, advertising, and physical distribution under a vice president of marketing who normally has no specific product-line responsibilities. Competition between Toshiba and Hitachi has recently centered on financing services; both companies have been strengthening their finance subsidiaries, which specialize in offering credit to customers on behalf of individual operating divisions.

Distributors are a fine example of marketing resources shared among multiple manufacturers. Many Japanese home appliance manufacturers have service outlets capable of repairing both white and brown goods.

Outside of marketing, shared resources are often observed in R&D, in the form of technical licensing and joint development. Where the key function does not lie in technology, or where technology cannot be monopolized, licensing is usually a more sensible way of lowering development costs. When development costs are exceptionally high, transnational R&D efforts may even be undertaken to help a company remain competitive in the worldwide market. Aircraft (the Airbus), atomic reactors (the BWR consortium comprising GE, Hitachi, ASEA, and Toshiba), and off-shore drilling (in the North Sea and the Yellow Sea) are examples.

## Avoiding the pitfalls

Although sharing resources can lower specific functional costs, it does force a company to sacrifice the advantages of concentrating on a specific business and/or market segment. The competition may attack this vulnerability by taking a more customized approach and using more sophisticated marketing techniques or better customer service in certain regions or segments. In particular, they may cherry-pick the lucrative segments or businesses. Hence, any company that chooses to share resources in order to lower certain functional costs needs to be very sure that it has an alert group of strategists in charge of marketing and competitive analyses.

Omron Tateishi Electronics, for example, uses a powerful pooled sales force to distribute a wide variety of electromechanical and electronic components. More than half of these components eventually find their way into eight kinds of end products—including game machines, audiovisual equipment, machine tools, and automobiles —either directly, by sale to the final-assembly manufacturers, or indirectly through subassembly vendors.

Some time ago, having discovered that its competitors were beginning to concentrate on fewer large-volume components, Omron installed two types of managers: (1) a manager charged with keeping watch on specific competitors, and (2) eight market managers responsible for analyzing trends in given end-use markets, specialized competitors' moves, and customization needs. These managers, who have no line responsibilities, act as sources of additional information and direction to compensate for the limitations of the shared sales force.

For Omron to have reorganized its entire sales force around the competition or around specific end-use markets would have been uneconomical. Omron would no longer have been assured of a cost-structure advantage over the competition in a given product-market segment and would therefore have become vulnerable if the competition had chosen to fight segment by segment. By determinedly holding on to the cost advantage of its shared sales force, however, Omron has been able to profitably retain its share of more than 40 percent of the highly diversified components market.

Other things being equal, a lower-cost function can be a source of profit if the product is priced on a par with competition. If the cost differential is reflected in the price, it can be a means of expanding market share.

# 11
# Competitor-Based Strategies

As we have just seen, there are several ways a company can go about reducing functional costs to become, or remain, economically competitive. That, however, is only one of several ways to develop strategies. In fact, there is a real trade-off to be made between the cost of a function and superiority in functional performance over a competitor.

Competitor-based strategies can be constructed by looking at possible sources of differentiation in functions ranging from purchasing, design, and engineering to sales and servicing. The main point to remember is that any difference between you and your competitors must be related to one or more of the three elements that jointly determine profit: price, volume, and cost. If, for example, you can get a better price because of better design, you may be able to achieve better profit performance than your competitors.

Even if your price and unit costs are identical to those of your competitors, you may be able to gain a bigger share of the market if you have more outlets. Figure 11–1 illustrates a convenient way (termed "leakage analysis") of systematically exhausting the possible areas of difference between you and your competitors. Clearly, differences that are unfavorable to you can cause you to lose certain fractions of the total market.

For example, certain customer segments may have "leaked" away from you because you are not offering the right product or model. The obvious remedy—expanding your product range—may or may not be feasible, depending on the relative competence of your engineering force or whether your production facilities and people are flexible enough to accommodate a wider range of models without losing economic competitiveness.

Other leakages may represent the customers your salespeople never encounter. Still another cause may be product image. Perhaps your competitor's advertising has been so effective that customers go out of their way to look for the competitor's product. Or it may be a matter of sheer mathematical probability. If your competitor's distribution network is much denser than your own, he will naturally be able to capture more customers.

In order to increase your share of market, you need to stop unnecessary leakage as best you can. Expanding your market coverage in terms of sales force or number of outlets may seem a quick way of reducing leakage, but it normally costs a lot of money. Before taking this course, therefore, it is important to make sure that your winning ratio (ratio of successful sales to total customers competed for) is high enough to justify the investment. If it is not fairly high, the probability is that additional coverage of the market would bring in only very modest incremental growth in share, and the cost of increasing the coverage will not be justified.

Now let us explore how differences between your company and its competition—whether they are differences in product and services as perceived by customers, in cost, or in functional competence—can influence overall corporate results. We can begin by examining some examples of competitor-based strategies in more detail.

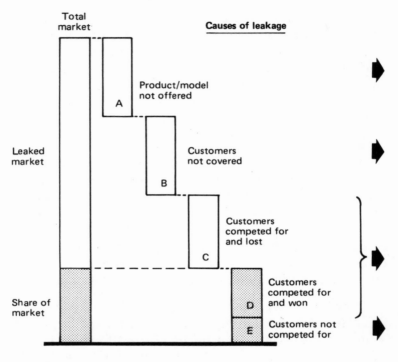

Useful definitions:   Share of market = D + E
Winning ratio = D/(C + D)
Market coverage = C + D + E
Product range = B + C + D + E
Cream skimming factor = (Winning ratio)/(Share of market) = 1/(C/D + 1) (E/D + 1)

**Figure 11-1**   Possible sources of competitive differentiation.

## The power of an image

Consider the case of Sony. For a long time Sony enjoyed a superior quality image in the United States which enabled it to price its color TVs much higher than the competition. In Japan, however, this was not the case, and Sony products were priced at parity with those of Matsushita (Panasonic) and others. Much the same situation pre-

| Possible areas of differentiation | Possible means |
|---|---|
| **Product range** ........ | ● Engineering flexibility<br>● Manufacturing technology |
| **Customer's own initiatives** ............<br>**Distribution** ...........<br>**Sales force** ............ | ● Image/reputation<br>● Network density<br>● Disciplined call pattern |
| **Product** .............<br>**Sales force** ...........<br>**Service** ..............<br>**Finance** ............. | ● Performance and/or price, availability<br>● Training<br>● Image/cost/performance<br>● Payment terms |
| **Relationship** ......... | ● Captive arrangement |

vailed in the case of Honda's passenger cars (Civic, Accord, and Prelude). Both Sony and Honda invested more heavily in public relations and promotion and managed these functions more carefully than did their competitors. The resulting image difference was reflected in a price premium, typically 5 to 10 percentage points, that enabled both companies to outsell their competitors with equivalent product performance.

Max Factor has a much better quality image in Japan than its larger U.S. competitors, simply because it has managed the marketing functions, especially promotion and distribution, with much greater care. Yamaha and Nikon, too, adopted strategies built on a superior quality image. Nikon, however, relied on its image too long and was caught off balance when Olympus introduced its small, lightweight single-lens reflex (SLR), Canon introduced electronic exposure control, and Konica brought in automatic loading, winding, and focusing. In all these cases, Nikon's competitors shifted the battleground from image to technology.

When product performance and mode of distribution are very difficult to differentiate, image may be the only source of positive differentiation. But as the case of the Swiss watch industry reminds us, a strategy built on image can be risky and must be monitored constantly. Moreover, because of differences in culture and in mass-media structure, image differentials may not travel across national boundaries.

As we saw in Chapter 4, Sakura film lost share to Fuji in Japan because its association with *sakura* (cherry blossoms) suggests an image that is pinkish, vague, and soft, whereas Fuji is naturally associated with green trees, blue sky, and the brilliant snowcap of Mount Fuji. Interestingly enough, Fuji even chose green for the color of its box (Sakura's is red) and deliberately stressed its green image. Although they could see no difference in "blind" tests, people were somehow led to believe that Sakura's prints were perceptibly reddish.

Once a company is locked into this kind of image, it is very difficult to change without changing the brand name and identity altogether, and that usually means starting from scratch. Yet retaining the current image will result in a vicious cycle—a declining market share leading to a still poorer customer image, leading in turn to further loss of market share, and so on. In an extreme case, however, a manufacturer may in fact choose to stay with an image he would prefer to shed. Exxon still calls itself

"Esso" in Japan for the very good reason that the sound *xo* is the Japanese equivalent of an English word not freely used in polite society even today.

## Exploiting tangible advantages

Often, of course, a company can choose to fight on the basis of its real functional strengths, as the case of Toyota illustrates. Recognizing that service is a critical factor to forklift truck customers, Toyota chose it as the major battleground. This was an important strategic decision, since it entailed high fixed costs—so high that Toyota's subcritical competitors could not afford to match its investment. Today Toyota's forklift truck business has an awesome service network; the company boasts that it can dispatch a service car to any part of Japan within two hours. As a result, despite its rather conventional product and pricing schemes, Toyota's share of this service-hungry industry continues to climb.

Likewise, customer relationships can be a source of differentiation. Japanese bureaucrats, who retire at age 55, need a second career opportunity. It is public knowledge that a corporation providing reasonable positions with acceptable security for these retiring high-ranking officers gets special privileges in public bidding in ways ranging from early access to bid information to influencing the public decision makers by leveraging the senior position the officer formerly held in the bureau in charge. The number of high military officers who used to retire to top management positions in the U.S. defense industry indicates that this latter phenomenon is not confined to Japan.

Many Japanese automobile manufacturers fully exploit their relationships with employees' families, relatives, and friends as well as their superior bargaining power with component vendors and subcontractors. Larger companies tend to have a natural advantage over smaller companies in exploiting these kinds of relationships, which explains why the "Big Three"—Toyota, Nissan, and Mitsubishi—put so much emphasis on sales to insiders.

Needless to say, positive differentiation alone does not automatically amount to a good strategy. The advantage it confers must be persistently deployed over competitors who are unable to close the gap and will therefore be losers in the battle for customers.

### Capitalizing on profit- and cost-structure differences

If the competition has a clear cost advantage and chooses to reflect it in price, a company with a higher cost structure is doomed to fail if it resorts to mere cutthroat warfare. It must find other ways of fighting; in other words, it must search for functional differentiation, as we have already noted.

But what about situations in which the two competing companies have significantly different cost and/or profit structures? One possibility is to fully exploit the economic structural difference without regard to the third party in the strategic triangle: the customer.

First, the difference in sources of profit might be exploited. Suppose Company A is making all its profit from servicing and none from new equipment sales, while the reverse is true for Company B. Company A could still lower its equipment price to wipe out Company B's profit. Service in any industry—be it trucks, machinery, or office equipment—is a relatively captive, stable business compared with sales of new equipment. Hence, Company A is a good deal less likely to lose servicing to its competitor, even though Company B might lower its service charges in retaliation, than B is to lose sales of new equipment to A.

Second, a difference in the ratio of fixed cost to variable cost might also be exploited strategically. Suppose a vertically integrated and automated Company C has a higher fixed-cost ratio than Company D, which purchases basic components from outside. Company D can lower prices in a sluggish market and win market share. This hurts Company C, because the market price is too low to justify its high-fixed-cost–low-volume operation. Conversely, when the market recovers and demand is strong, Company D should raise its price above that of Company C so as to earn a maximum profit, given the supply bottleneck resulting from Company C's limited and fixed production capacity.

Third, a similar (though in one way significantly different) approach might be exploited by a small company in competition with a giant. By virtue of its size, the larger company will have the natural advantage of so-called economies of scale, resulting primarily from better utilization of fixed costs, whether in engineering, plant, or advertising. For the small company to fight on the basis of a fixed-cost strategy would be a losing proposition, because a certain critical mass of fixed investment is required to be competitive; if that critical mass is divided by the annual turnover, the larger company naturally has a lower cost as a percentage of sales. Hence, if it is at all possible, the small company should try to fight on the basis of variable costs, which by definition are proportional to sales and therefore do not necessarily represent a natural handicap for a small competitor.

## Tactics for flyweights

For example, to influence the consumer's brand selection, a small cosmetic company might offer more elegant containers and more elaborate packaging (variable costs) rather than trying to gain an advantage through TV commercials. If the company should choose to compete in mass-media advertising, additional fixed costs will absorb such a large portion of its revenue that its giant competitors will inevitably win. Likewise, a massive R&D effort to develop a new deodorant would be a fixed-cost game and therefore unwise for a small company unless its research goal is precisely defined and looks readily attainable.

The same concept can be applied to structuring dealer incentives. To protect their dominant position in the home appliance market, Japan's top three home appliance companies—Matsushita, Toshiba, and Hitachi—pay incentives in strict proportion to their captive dealers' total sales in yen. Any competitor with significantly smaller volume trying to match or outdo the top three on that basis has lost out before it starts.

One company, however, decided to calculate its incentives on a graduated percentage basis rather than on absolute volume, thus making the incentives variable by guaranteeing the dealer a larger percentage of each extra appliance sold. The Big Three, of course, cannot afford to offer such high percentages across the board to their respective franchised stores; their profitability would soon be eroded if they did.

Utilizing the structural difference between fixed and variable costs will not necessarily enable a smaller company to gain a positive strategic advantage, but it can often help reduce a severe handicap vis-à-vis giant competitors. In this case the smaller appliance maker appears to have been successful in living parasitically, as it were, off its giant competitor. Brute strength is not always required to survive in an encounter with a heavyweight.

# 12
# Corporate Strategy

So far we have been examining the elements of strategy for a single business. Most companies, of course, have more than one business, and a large corporation today may have 100 or more distinctively different businesses. Viewed from the center, the strategy of conglomerates and diversified companies therefore needs to address two questions:

1. How should the individual business be integrated into the total corporation?

2. Is there, or should there be, a strategy at the corporate level that is different from the sum of the component strategies of the individual businesses?

To find the answers, we need to look again at three concepts: the corporation, the business, and management resources.

## What is a corporation?

The postwar history of American business is a history of confusion in the very definition of the term "corporation" and of consequent confusion in corporate strategy itself. Many articles and books purporting to deal with corporate strategy have in fact dealt only with business strategy or at best with the strategy of companies such as Xerox or Polaroid at a time when they were virtually single-product companies.

There are really three kinds of corporations: single-product, conglomerate, and diversified. The strategy of a single-product company that is not planning to diversify is identical with business unit strategy as discussed in the last three chapters. Conglomerates and diversified corporations, however, are each a very different matter. While the conglomerate tries to maximize the wealth of the stockholder by such financial measures as resource allocation, especially allocation of funds, the diversified company goes a step further. It tries to maximize the wealth of the corporation by exploiting synergies (cross-fertilization of strengths) between its various businesses.

For example, General Electric's power generation and transmission product lines, such as switchgears and transformers, are distributed through the company's mighty pooled sales force, which reaches virtually every utility company in the nation. Matsushita Electric, Japan's largest and strongest home appliance company, sells products ranging from stereo equipment to white goods through a single distribution network. Hitachi has several very large laboratories engaged in basic research in electronics. Operating divisions engaged in such diversified businesses as computers, consumer electronics, and industrial robots can all benefit from the LSI and sensor technologies developed by these central R&D laboratories.

As these examples illustrate, a diversified company differs fundamentally from a conglomerate in that it is organized to (1) exploit its latent functional synergies to achieve cost and quality leadership over its single-business competitors, and (2) use its superior and deeper understanding of the business and its individual key factors for success to gain an edge over its conglomerate competitors. Such functional strengths, found as commonalities applicable to various businesses, include mass-production technology, design turnaround time, R&D, mass distribution channels, corporate image, and the like. All offer opportunities for cross-fertilization.

A diversified company that has no such synergy across various businesses is nothing more than a conglomerate managing an assortment of discrete businesses. Financial management and human resource allocation tend, therefore, to become the only justifiable roles of corporate headquarters.

A conglomerate can be seen as an exalted investment portfolio manager, dedicated to maximizing overall return on investment over the long term. As such, it may acquire an electronics company for long-term growth, an insurance company for cash flow, a fast-food chain for short-term growth, and a pharmaceutical company for short- to medium-term return. None of these businesses is related to the others, except that they constitute collectively a convenient vehicle for a self-contained capital management system. A conglomerate, as such, will have a difficult time in trying to define its corporate objective in other than financial or numerical terms, such as "maximize ROI" or "achieve 15 percent annual EPS growth." Seen from the center, the nature of a conglomerate limits its purpose to the making of money, and this is probably as it should be.

A serious and fundamental problem, however, has arisen on the U.S. business scene from the fact that corporate objectives of this kind have progressively invaded the realm of diversified companies and single-business companies, particularly the former. Figure 12–1 illustrates how the predominant focus of management concern be-

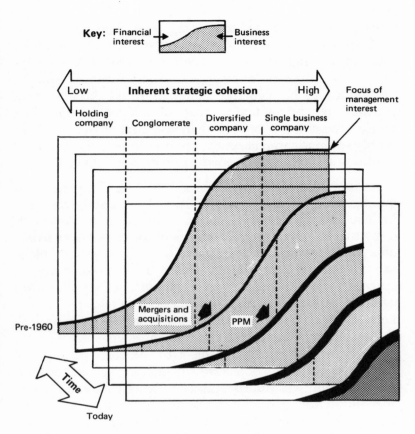

**Key:** Financial interest → | | ← Business interest

Low ←── **Inherent strategic cohesion** ──→ High

Focus of management interest

Holding company | Conglomerate | Diversified company | Single business company

Mergers and acquisitions

PPM

Pre-1960

Time

Today

***Figure 12–1*** The growing dominance of financial objectives.

tween conglomerates and diversified companies has been shifting from business to financial considerations.

This shift has gained momentum as mergers and acquisitions have become a popular mode of growth through diversification. Since it is hard for any acquired company to meld its corporate culture and value system with those of the acquirer, diversified corporations with many acquired companies among their operating divisions have understandably tended to give up, over time, the hope of genuinely integrating the resources and value systems of the acquired companies into their own. This lack of unifying forces across their businesses has caused diversified companies to behave like conglomerates. Accelerating the drift away from the traditional business orientation, many diversified companies turned during the 1970s to highly sophisticated corporate planning models and techniques such as product portfolio management (PPM).

As its name suggests, PPM is based on the concept of managing an investment portfolio. It is a tool for optimizing the overall corporate objective function, be it growth or return on investment, under constraints such as available funds or number of employees. Individual businesses are graphically represented as dots on a four- or nine-cell matrix, located according to (1) the attractiveness (often equated with growth and total size) of the respective markets in which they are competing (vertical axis) and (2) the estimated strength of each business vis-à-vis its competitors in that market. Subject to the corporation's assumed overriding objective of achieving an overall portfolio that will appropriately balance risk and return, specific strategic implications are associated with particular positions on the matrix (Figure 12-2).

For example, all else being equal, an aggressive investment strategy is considered suitable for a strong business in a highly attractive market, while a moderately strong business in a declining industry would be considered a candidate for "harvesting," or managing for cash, unless there is some way to "shift the dot" to a more promising position on the matrix through management action.

In this sort of context, an individual business tends to degenerate into an impersonal dot on the portfolio matrix, characterized only by static, quantifiable measures

| Market attractiveness | | | |
|---|---|---|---|
| **High** | **Serious entry into the market**<br><br>Opportunistic position to test growth prospects; withdraw if indications of sustainable growth are lacking. | **Selective growth**<br><br>Select areas where strength can be maintained, and concentrate investment in those areas. | **All-out struggle**<br><br>Concentrate entire effort on maintaining strength; if necessary maintain profit structure by investment. |
| **Medium** | **Limited expansion or withdrawal**<br><br>Look for ways of achieving expansion without high risk; if unsuccessful, withdraw before involved too deeply. | **Selective expansion**<br><br>Concentrate investment, and expand only in segments where profitability is good and risk is relatively low. | **Maintenance of superiority**<br><br>Build up ability to counter competition, avoiding large-scale investment; emphasize profitability by raising productivity. |
| **Low** | **Loss-minimizing**<br><br>Prevent losses before they occur by avoiding investment and by lowering fixed costs; when loss is unavoidable, withdraw. | **Overall harvesting**<br><br>Promote switch from fixed to variable costs; emphasize profitability through VA and VE of variable costs. | **Limited harvesting**<br><br>Reduce degree of risk to a minimum in several segments; emphasize profit by protecting profitability even if loss of market position is involved. |
| | Low | Medium | High |
| | ← | Corporate strengths | → |

*Figure 12–2* Nine specimen standardized strategies.

of market attractiveness and business strength. The relative attractiveness of Business A to Business B becomes the sole basis for allocating corporate resources. While this technique imposes a valuable discipline of objectivity and impartiality, it tends to neglect the important success factors such as creativity, imagination, and persistence. And these traits, of course, are determined very largely by the talents and temperament of the person in charge, whose style sets the tone and focus of the business. If he does not personally display these traits or reward subordinates who do, these patterns of behavior will wither and die within the business.

The value of any system depends on how it is employed, and PPM—which has been much criticized by people who haven't really used or worked at it—is no exception. If care is taken to understand the reasons for the position of the dot, and if the matrix is used to generate creative ideas on each business, given its situation relative to other businesses in the corporate context, PPM can be very useful. Too many corporate executives and planners, however, are in so much of a hurry to climb the corporate ladder that they can't spare the time to understand each business in their diversified "portfolios." In their hands, PPM, which was originally conceived as a device for determining priorities for an investment portfolio, has been perverted into a device for killing certain businesses and boosting others, purely in order to maximize the corporation's financial results. Thus, the PPM approach has further pushed the focus of management concern toward purely financial measures and hastened the conglomeratization of diversified companies in the United States.

This attenuation of the business focus has been going on for more than a decade. To reverse it, the diversified company must be seen as a coherent assembly of businesses and managed accordingly. This means defining the role of corporate headquarters as extracting functional synergies and/or strategically deploying the benefits of shared resources among the constituent businesses. As pictured in Figure 12–3, such a diversified company would ideally comprise five conceptual levels, possibly though not necessarily reflected in its overall organization structure.

The lowest level, product-market segments, comprises

the smallest units that can engage in competition. Hence, it has critical strategic value. If "shampoos," for example, constitutes a strategic planning unit (SPU; the second layer up), shampoos for babies and dandruff-remover shampoos would each constitute a product-market segment.

The SPU level ("shampoos"—or more correctly, as we shall presently see, "hair washing") is convenient for developing business strategy, because an SPU can logically have its own engineering, production, and sales functions. But whether it functions as an independent operating and execution unit as well as a planning unit or is grouped with others in a strategic business unit (SBU) depends on two considerations.

The first is sheer economics. In order to gain cost leadership in the industry, certain functions should be shared among different SPUs if there are potentially effective commonalities. To examine the impact of such synergies, one needs to develop hypothetical cost structures and estimate the net difference of each functional cost item as between freestanding and lumped-together SPUs. Figure 12–4 illustrates a typical case, demonstrating the interrelationships between SPUs and strategic business units, the third layer. Of the investments required, Type 2 and Type 4 engines can be developed through almost identical R&D efforts, the only difference being in minor application devices. Likewise, Types 1 and 2 are distributed through the same channel, and there is good potential synergy between these two businesses. Hence, lumping together these SPUs saves $6 million over the cost of four freestanding SPUs, such as we might find in a loosely coupled diversified company with no coordination between different SPUs, or in four different single-business competitors.

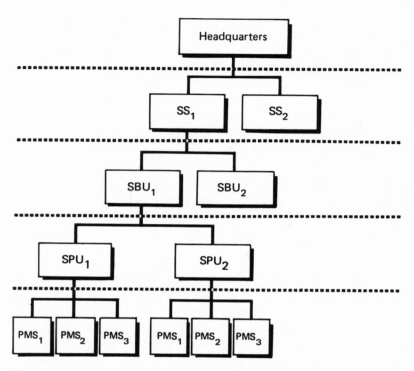

***Figure 12–3*** Five-layer concept of a diversified company.

The second decisive consideration for the formation of an SBU is management's commitment to and concentration on a given business. Lumping certain SPUs together may gain synergy at too great a cost if management attention and commitment to the individual businesses is thereby dissipated.

For example, three SPUs, concerned respectively with shampoo, soap, and toothpaste, might be put together in a "toiletries" SBU, since all three businesses use the same distribution network and could thus have a pooled

**Purpose of unit**

| | |
|---|---|
| **Corporate headquarters** | . Corporate goal-setting<br>. Culture/systems<br>. Resource procurement |
| ■■■■■■■■■■■■■■■■■■■■■■ | |
| **Strategic sector** | . Long-term strategic planning and resource allocation<br>. Socio-political unit |
| ■■■■■■■■■■■■■■■■■■■■■■ | |
| **Strategic business unit** | . Mid- to short-term strategy execution<br>. Functional synergy |
| ■■■■■■■■■■■■■■■■■■■■■■ | |
| **Strategic planning unit** | . Basic business planning unit (product-market strategy)<br>. May have some functional autonomy |
| ■■■■■■■■■■■■■■■■■■■■■■ | |
| **Product-market segment** | . Meaningful differentiation unit<br>. Smallest unit to encounter competition |

sales force. This SBU would be an operational rather than a business planning unit, because individual business strategies would still have to be developed around SPUs and product-market segments. But suppose the SBU head, as an operating executive, ignores the subtle differences between soap and other toiletries, e.g., its suitability for gift purposes, or the institutional needs of factories and hotels. Lacking the in-depth knowledge and concentrated attention of a manager whose whole concern is selling soap, the soap business within the toiletry SBU may begin losing sales to its specialized competition.

| Basic strategy | Generate maximum profit from Type 4 engine and invest in Type 3 for aggressive growth. Selective growth for other engines. |
|---|---|
| Basic actions | Maintain high price for Type 4 engine. Expand export of Type 2 and seek OEM for Type 3 combined with subsidiary A's engines. Expand export of Type 1, but stop Series X development if and when it proves unprofitable. |

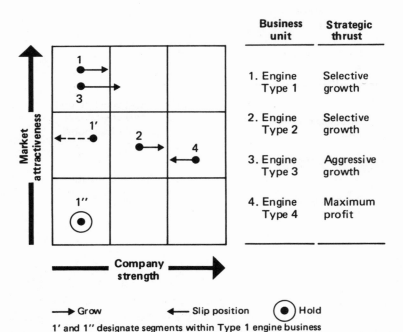

| Business unit | Strategic thrust |
|---|---|
| 1. Engine Type 1 | Selective growth |
| 2. Engine Type 2 | Selective growth |
| 3. Engine Type 3 | Aggressive growth |
| 4. Engine Type 4 | Maximum profit |

⟶ Grow    ⟵ Slip position    (●) Hold

1' and 1'' designate segments within Type 1 engine business

*Figure 12–4*  Grouping business units as an SBU to exploit potential synergies.

Should this happen, it will be clear that the SBU grouping, though aimed at achieving cost leadership, has only hindered the healthy growth of the soap business. Thus

| Labor absorption | Sales | Profit | Share of market (%) | Export ratio (%) | R&D | Investment | |
|---|---|---|---|---|---|---|---|
| | | | | | | Production | Distribution |
| 690 | 141 | 4 | 7 | 35 | 0 | 2 | 3 |
| 450 | 186 | 23 | 18 | 42 | 3 | 2 | (3) |
| 1450 | 300 | 15 | 25 | 50 | 3 | 0 | 0 |
| 1000 | 207 | 10 | 15 | 77 | (3) | 8 | 0 |
| 3590 | 834 | 44 | 23 | 52 | 6 | 12 | 3 |

○ Double counting for synergy

it may make sense to dismantle the SBU and let each individual SPU fight against its own well-defined enemy.

In order to determine whether an SBU should be an execution unit (and hence, probably, an operating division), sophisticated management judgment must be brought to bear on the trade-off between the cost leadership achievable through synergy and the value of management concentration on each of the proposed constituent SPUs as compared with major competitors. In short, an SBU is essentially an execution-oriented unit, and the purpose of planning at the SBU level should only be to develop effective functional strategies for sharing resources to obtain the desired synergies. Hence, the planning horizon of an SBU is seldom more than three to five years. Management should continually monitor the strategic appropriateness of its SBU groupings, since they can swiftly be outmoded by changes in industry structure or in the relative weight of major cost elements. Their relevance can also be eroded by strategic moves on the part of competitors, possibly including reorganization.

In concept, a strategic sector (SS), the fourth-level unit, would encompass several SBUs. It can be thought of as an organizational unit whose function is to allocate corporate resources over the longer term, say five to ten years. For example, a "toiletries" SBU might be grouped with a "dishes" and a "tissues" SBU in a strategic sector labeled "consumer disposables." Or if it also encompassed hardware such as kitchen gadgets and plastic buckets, the strategic sector might be labeled "consumer sundries." As such, it would be positioned conceptually against other possible sectors—e.g., home appliances, furniture, lighting, or audiovisual equipment—under a single corporate umbrella.

A large diversified company may, in fact, encompass all of these. If so, its *corporate* objective—i.e., the common objective of its component sectors—might be to deliver comfort to every household or to provide the best household convenience and efficiency products (other than food). A company like this—call it the Consumer

Household Corporation—will need to reallocate people and funds flexibly in response to changes in the sociopolitical environment, gross national product (GNP) mix, living standards, consumers' habits, use of disposable income and of leisure time, quality-of-life aspirations, and levels of sophistication and luxury.

Such changes are gradual. Our Consumer Household Corporation need not reexamine them every year. But over a five- to ten-year period, there will be marked differences in each of these elements. Thus it makes sense to use the strategic sector as a long-range planning unit, though not necessarily as an execution and operation unit. For example, if consumer interests are gradually shifting from cleanliness and personal care to culture and social prestige, top corporate management might decide to emphasize furniture and audiovisual equipment rather than toiletries and sundry hardware.

Because our Consumer Household Corporation is embedded in the culture and value system of society, in some sense it is inherently in touch with consumers' needs. This doesn't mean that it can afford to dispense with market research. More important, however, everyone in the corporation is (or ought to be) interested in the day-to-day existence of average people and honestly eager to improve it by offering better household products.

It is this philosophical backbone, together with the interwoven and synergistic nature of its constituent businesses, which differentiates a true diversified company from a conglomerate. Such a company cannot succeed over the long term if it tries to manage its businesses purely from a financial point of view. Financial indexes are measures of success in its pursuit of its corporate objectives; they cannot be the objectives of the corporation per se. By contrast, a conglomerate, which lacks

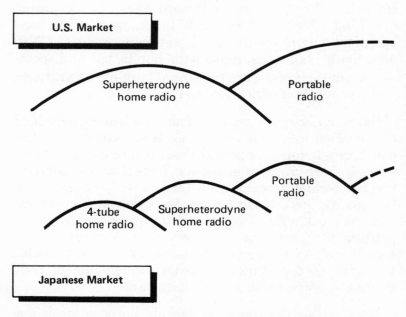

**Figure 12–5** Product-development history of the radio.

these interwoven philosophies, can treat its diversified businesses as discrete opportunities and means for achieving a quantified financial corporate objective.

## Business versus product

With this concept of a corporation in mind, let us return to our definition of the "business." The reader may by now be wondering why I chose to use the term "strategic planning unit" instead of "product line" in Figure 12–3. Shampoos are certainly a product line, but the *business* a shampoo maker is in is to provide a means for washing hair. Likewise, radios are a product line, but the business is audio information and/or entertainment. Figure 12–5 illustrates one effect of this difference of perception.

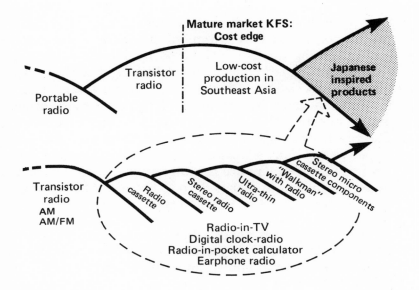

Many financially oriented, diversified U.S. electrical manufacturers treated radios as a species of hardware: in other words, essentially as a dot on a product portfolio matrix. Convinced that every product line has its natural "product life cycle," they treated the radio as a product that had passed its peak and the radio business as a prime candidate for financial "milking" or "harvesting." Chronically starved of investment funds and management talent, a product line called "radio" accordingly lived out its natural life. This was a prime example of a self-fulfilling prophecy.

Japanese radio manufacturers, however, didn't treat radios as a hardware-oriented product line. They focused not on the product but on the category of goods into which it fell. Instead of blindly accepting the assumptions that (1) every product has its life cycle and (2) the business they were in was radios, they created demand, using the concept of audio entertainment based on consumers' basic listening needs. Untroubled by the idea that the radio as hardware had peaked out, they studied the times, places, and occasions of such consumer behavior as listening to broadcasts, recording, and listening to recorded music, and they drew an entirely different conclusion. The resulting floods of composite products, such as radio cassettes and Sony's Walkman, are history. The fact that American consumers are actually buying these products in such numbers is decisive proof that user needs, latent or explicit, were there all the time.

The crucial point, then, is how you define the business and how you treat it. If you really believe in a product's value and are emotionally committed to it, you will not take an outsider's view of it, the way a portfolio manager using "objective" indexes might do. A business reflects its manager. If you see yourself as the ultimate controller of your business's fate, you can prolong its life by adapting your products and services to fit the user's changing needs within the broad, categorical definition of the business you have chosen to adopt.

In fact, it is how they do it rather than what industries they are in that distinguishes the best-performing businesses. Even in the fastest-growing industries, such as facsimile, office computers, and fast food, there are many losers. At least in Japan, high-growth industries tend to attract too many entrants, just as the Yukon attracted too many gold prospectors. For example, there are thirteen participants in Japan's $200 million facsimile market. Although it is growing at 35 percent annually, this allows less than a $20 million share per participant on average—hardly enough to compensate for the investments required to develop critical digital transmission technologies and sophisticated sales and service networks.

In fact, the emphasis of business planning has tended to shift in recent years from the vertical axis to the horizontal axis of the matrix, or company strength (Figure 12–6). The portfolio concept in the early days treated the two axes almost equivalently, but the conglomeratization of diversified companies during the 1970s led them gradually into an excessive preoccupation with the vertical axis. In a word, they became "gold seekers." Now that these companies have proved to themselves that they cannot build attractive businesses in attractive markets in competition with others who know the business better, the emphasis has been swinging toward the horizontal axis—company strength, or "how you do it."

The gold hunters' watchword may be "Invest to grow!" But how? Bystanders may urge more selectivity, but where, and to what extent? Answers to these questions can come only from profound understanding of the business. The value of such directional advice really hinges on what use is made of it and by whom. Management, after all, is people, and businesses are made successful by people, not by plans. Behind each success story in business are men and women who conceived the ideas, developed the strategies, and executed the planned actions. It is my conviction that throughout the 1980s there will be a healthy revival of entrepreneurs who will demonstrate once again how crucially the success of a business depends on the way it is managed.

While there is no question that high-growth industries offer better opportunities, even in a good industry a company cannot achieve a stable leadership position if it is managed solely from a financial point of view. And, as can

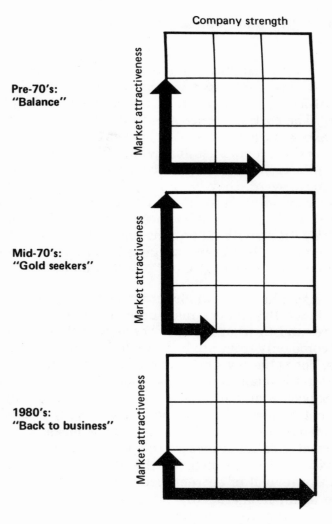

*Figure 12–6* Psychological evolution of product portfolio management.

be seen in Figure 12–7, some companies can grow fast and make money in the most depressed industries.

BUILDING SUCCESSFUL STRATEGIES

Indeed, there are ways of making money for a surprisingly long time in a bad industry, so long as a reasonable level of demand remains. Kanzaki Seishi is doing exceptionally well in the deeply troubled Japanese pulp and paper industry by achieving a high-value-added operation through low inventory and transportation costs and through shifting its product mix toward the high end of the market.

Within a given industry, there are usually 7 to 12 percentage points of performance spread among companies in a given category of operating cost. Thus, as Figure 12–8 shows, the best performer (Company A) in a depressed industry can earn profits comparable to those of the worst performer (Company B) in an industry with operating margins 15 percentage points higher. A similar phenomenon can be seen in American industry.*

## Management resources

"Resource allocation" normally means allocating available funds. Corporate resources, however, include much more than money. A favorite phrase of Japanese business planners is *hito-kane-mono,* or people, money, and things (fixed assets). They believe that streamlined corporate management is achieved when these three critical resources are in balance, without any superfluity or waste (Figure 12–9). For example, cash over and beyond what competent people can intelligently expend is wasted. Again, too many managers without enough money will exhaust their energies and involve their colleagues in time-wasting paper warfare over the allocation of the limited funds.

---

* See William K. Hall, "Survival Strategies in a Hostile Environment," *Harvard Business Review,* vol. 58, no. 5 September-October 1980, pp. 75–85.

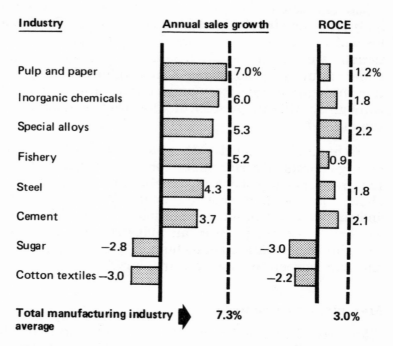

**Figure 12-7** High performers in depressed Japanese industries. *[Based on data from Bank of Japan; annual reports (Yukashoken Hokokusho).]*

Of the three critical resources, funds should be allocated last. Based on the available *mono*—plant, machinery, technology, process know-how, functional strengths, and so on—the corporation should first allocate management talent. Once these *hito* have developed creative, imaginative ideas to capture the business's upward potential, the *kane,* or money, should be allocated to the specific ideas and programs generated by individual managers.

Even within the context of PPM, funds should not be allocated simply because the business is in an attractive category. They should be invested in attractive programs

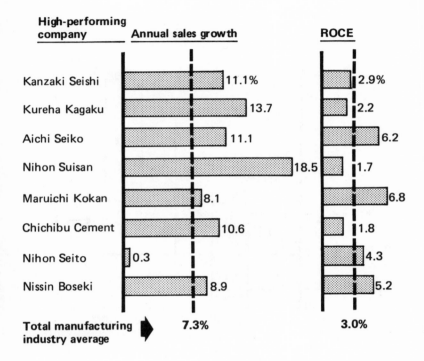

| High-performing company | Annual sales growth | ROCE |
|---|---|---|
| Kanzaki Seishi | 11.1% | 2.9% |
| Kureha Kagaku | 13.7 | 2.2 |
| Aichi Seiko | 11.1 | 6.2 |
| Nihon Suisan | 18.5 | 1.7 |
| Maruichi Kokan | 8.1 | 6.8 |
| Chichibu Cement | 10.6 | 1.8 |
| Nihon Seito | 0.3 | 4.3 |
| Nissin Boseki | 8.9 | 5.2 |
| **Total manufacturing industry average** | 7.3% | 3.0% |

rather than attractive industries. As we have seen, imaginative planning and execution in depressed industries can bring better returns than poorly planned and executed operations in good industries. Only good people can generate good ideas, and only good managers can execute good strategies. Funds are a means of accomplishing the corporate goal, the centripetal force that pulls together and unites the three critical management resources.

A diversified company can redeploy not only its managers but its workers, engineers, and sales force as well. For example, throughout the inflationary 1970s, Hitachi, a

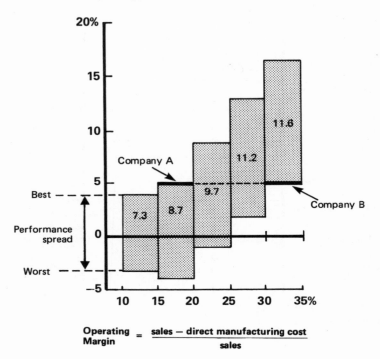

*Figure 12–8* Operating performance of Japanese chemical companies. *[Based on data from Nikkei Handbook of Management Indices (1980).]*

diversified electrical and electronics manufacturer, has been shifting its engineering resources from industrial and power-generation businesses to information-based businesses such as electronic components (e.g., LSI) and computers while managing a decline in its total work force (Figure 12–10).

Likewise, factory workers can be made into sales and service workers, and in some instances even into programmers, if appropriate attention and efforts are paid to

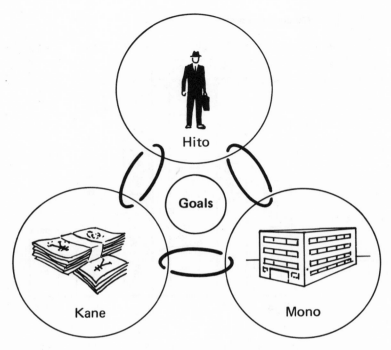

***Figure 12–9*** Management's key resources: the Japanese view.

their retraining. NEC, Japan's largest producer of communications equipment and electronic devices, has moved further and further away from its traditional heavy reliance on government as a customer and into sales of standard products to industry; in the process, it has shifted a large number of its workers into selling to industry (Figure 12–11). Although extensive automation in production made many jobs superfluous, the total number of employees was kept constant—no mean feat in Japan, where large corporations do not lay off or fire workers.

We can see that each of these companies is shifting critical human resources over a long time horizon, with

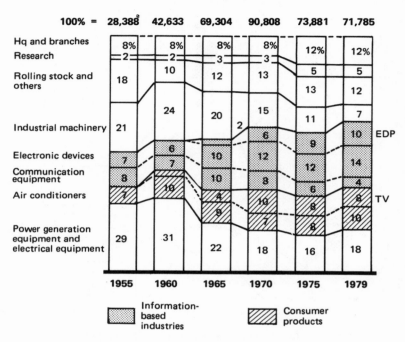

**Number of employees, by division**

**Figure 12-10** Hitachi shifts its people mix. *[Based on data from Yukashoken Hokokusho; Hitachi and Matsushita (by Okamoto).]*

a particular corporate goal in mind. Hitachi's reallocation of resources seems to be aimed at shifting the business mix into higher-value-added industries and away from direct cost competition with companies based elsewhere in Southeast Asia, while in NEC's case the goal is evidently to play a major role in combining the computer and communications industries.

High-performing companies such as Hitachi and NEC seem to do very well at developing long-term strategy and organizing their business units for maximum synergy.

BUILDING SUCCESSFUL STRATEGIES

**NUMBER OF EMPLOYEES**

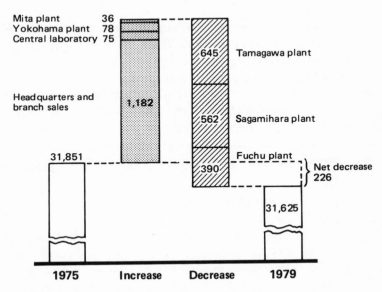

***Figure 12–11*** NEC's new emphasis on selling. *(Based on data from Yukashoken Hokokusho.)*

They also excel at execution. Through skillful resource allocation of *hito-kane-mono,* they balance this trinity of management functions to achieve superior results.

## Back to the corporation

Having explored the concepts of corporation, business, and resources, let's now return briefly to the questions posed at the outset about the role of the corporate level in strategy development. To answer the first question— how a collection of discrete businesses should be integrated into the total corporation—we can now say that a true diversified company should have a good strategic *raison d'être* for each of its businesses. Instead of managing its businesses as separate units, a large diversified company should seek to establish cost or quality leadership through synergies arising from shared functional resources. These businesses will then become stronger because they are parts of a corporation rather than freestanding single-business companies. Too many diversified companies strangle individual businesses with red tape in the form of financial and bureaucratic guidelines. Any synergy that may exist can be diluted, or even canceled, by the added complexities of managing the business interfaces with headquarters and other operating divisions.

What of the second question—the unique role of corporate headquarters above and beyond long-term resource procurement and allocation? The answer is that the corporate level has another vital function: to develop and install a corporatewide management system. The culture of the corporation tends to reflect the nature of corporate management systems strongly, particularly those systems relating to accounting and performance appraisal. Top management may be able to override the systems, but middle management must live with them. For this reason, management systems design and installation is a powerful though subtle device to set the pace and tone of the organization through a single common value system. Over time, management processes and systems tend to shape and form the culture of the corporation.

# Part 3
# Modern Strategic Realities

# 13
# Understanding the Economic Environment

Common sense should tell us that the most penetrating product-market analysis and the most imaginative applications of product portfolio management are worth little unless the strategist, in working them out, takes full and careful account of the broad currents of economic change that already seem certain to dominate the business environment of the 1980s. Accordingly, in this chapter we shall be looking at five key economic trends (Figure 13–1)—all marking, to some degree, significant changes from past decades—that will have an important impact on business strategies in the ten years ahead. They are:

¶ Continuing low growth

¶ Market maturity and strategic stalemate

¶ Uneven distribution of resources

¶ Growing international complexities

¶ Irreversible inflation

Obviously, the strategic thinker will do well to understand the background of each of these five factors, their implications for managers, and the ways in which corporate strategies should be shaped to take these implications into account. Let us consider each of them in turn.

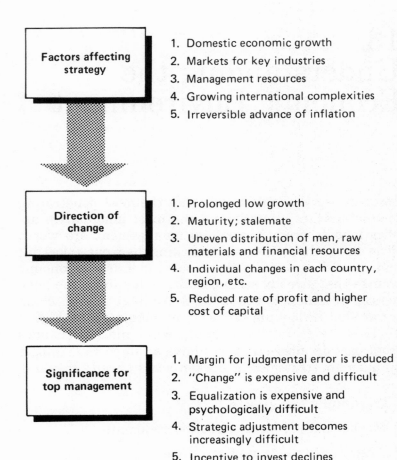

| Factors affecting strategy | 1. Domestic economic growth<br>2. Markets for key industries<br>3. Management resources<br>4. Growing international complexities<br>5. Irreversible advance of inflation |
| Direction of change | 1. Prolonged low growth<br>2. Maturity; stalemate<br>3. Uneven distribution of men, raw materials and financial resources<br>4. Individual changes in each country, region, etc.<br>5. Reduced rate of profit and higher cost of capital |
| Significance for top management | 1. Margin for judgmental error is reduced<br>2. "Change" is expensive and difficult<br>3. Equalization is expensive and psychologically difficult<br>4. Strategic adjustment becomes increasingly difficult<br>5. Incentive to invest declines |

**Figure 13–1** Fundamental changes in the business environment.

## Continuing low growth

It is not news that low economic growth is likely to continue. But not enough has been said in practical terms about the concrete changes in business activities that conditions of prolonged low growth require. We hear plenty of fine generalizations about new perspectives, but they do not often result in concrete, practical proposals.

Possibly the most alarming effect of low growth is the way it drastically limits the margin of error in managers' decisions and narrows the leeway within which mistakes in judgment can be accommodated. Overoptimism and other judgmental errors that frequently may escape serious penalty in times of prosperity may turn out to be catastrophically costly in a period of economic stagnation. This is why, directly after the 1973 oil crisis, some companies wisely conducted an urgent across-the-board examination of all the important managerial decisions they had taken over the previous ten years. The object: to screen out those which were no longer appropriate from those which were still valid in the new situation and then to make the corrections necessary to keep the company on course.

During a period of rapid economic growth, it is clearly important to be investing, even though it may not be clear how much investment is appropriate. Overinvestment is not a very serious worry, since the excess is likely to be absorbed in a year or two by the growth of the market. If the investment should prove insufficient, additional sums can be injected right away. Thus there is considerable room for errors of judgment.

By contrast, continuing low growth amplifies the painful consequences of strategic mistakes. Suddenly the market no longer forgives errors of judgment. This is why companies in which an ingrained skepticism toward accepted assumptions, the habit of analysis, and the practice of strategic thinking have become a way of life are the companies that seem to prosper so remarkably in bad times as well as good.

## Market maturity
## and strategic stalemate

A basic principle of marketing strategy today is that a company in a growing market should try to increase its share by investing in advance of market growth, accepting the increased risk for the sake of building its sales faster than the growth of the market. If all its competitors are participating to some extent in the growth of the market, a disproportionate gain in share by one company is a great deal less likely to provoke a backlash from the others.

When market growth slows down or stops, however—in other words, when a market reaches maturity—market shares more often than not become fixed, and competition approaches a condition of stalemate. In a stalemated market, where the market-share pattern has become rigid, customers' expectations and ideas about particular products tend to become rigid as well so that it becomes hard to stimulate additional new demand. Any change, in fact, becomes difficult and costly.

When a company takes various strategic steps to acquire a share of a mature product market, it often finds that the required investment far exceeds the gain. Experience has repeatedly shown that such moves as price reductions, advertising, and development of new products undertaken in this situation can almost always put profitability at risk.

Even maintaining a company's existing share may be expensive in a stalemated market. Usually a gradual widening takes place in the gap between companies with large shares and those with small shares. This is because the factors that enable companies to win a large share during the period of growth—vigorous investment in production facilities, expansion of sales networks, and introduction of new or improved products—often continue to operate as important management assets even after the emphasis of the strategy may have shifted from taking an aggressive approach to maintaining the company's present position. This is particularly noticeable in markets in which competition is centered on a single main product, such as beer, tires, cars, or motorcycles.

In a stalemated market, achieving growth in market share is costly not only for companies starting with a low market share but often for others as well. Sometimes companies that already have a large share may gain little from attempting to increase it, especially when their freedom of action is hampered by antitrust laws or consumer pressures. Yet no one, so far as I know, has yet come up with a really convincing, scientific method of cost-benefit analysis for evaluating the options available to a high-market-share company.

The best fundamental change of direction for a large-market-share company facing a strategic stalemate in which upward growth no longer pays would probably be to push for higher profits and invest them in other, more promising operations, e.g., diversification or opening up or developing overseas markets. Indeed, if its current market share is already at a level where further investment in existing operations is not going to pay, this may be the only logical alternative.

For a company that has taken its original or main business as far as it can go, diversification as a means of channeling surplus resources should certainly be considered. For the company which has not yet developed its main business to the full potential, however, diversification is probably one of the riskiest strategic choices that can be made. This is because management is dealing with two uncertainties—the market and the product to be off-ered—both representing markedly different key factors for success which the company may not possess today. Thus management should think twice, or possibly three times, before it tries to diversify.

What about publicly held companies that have already won a large market share and enjoy high profitability but have no intention either of opening up new markets or of diversifying? One option is to retire debt, but that is not a strategy for the long term. Another is simply to increase dividends. But this is difficult in Japan; it is argued that if this tactic were widely adopted, it could upset the stock market and make it harder for everyone, especially com-panies in a relatively weak position, to secure capital by floating stock issues.

What about companies in free competition whose mar-kets have matured and whose market share is stalemated —the situation that is likely to face most people responsi-ble for planning market strategy in the 1980s and beyond? For such companies there are various tactical options, e.g., increased advertising, price discounts, and concentration on specific geographical areas. But the cost-effectiveness of such moves is small, and they seldom bring about any dramatic increase in market share (al-though at one stage, when the market was growing, a company may well have gained and held a big increase in its share by vigorously pursuing some combination of these moves).

When the strategist is looking for solutions in a stale-mated market, one method is to challenge the conven-tional wisdom about product and market head-on. When the market was still growing, these commonsense as-sumptions or accepted ideas may have reflected the actu-al conditions for success accurately. Today they may be shackling the company's strategic potential. To break out of a market-share stalemate, the strategic thinker must sometimes have the courage to burst these shackles, even if it seems to mean flying in the face of common sense. (Challenging common sense isn't, of course, a surefire way of breaking a strategic stalemate, but clinging too long to the conventional wisdom *is* a reliable formula for failure!)

The color-generating system behind Sony's Trinitron picture tube, with its single electronic-beam gun, challenged the common sense of the industry, which had always used three electronic guns for the three primary colors. It was in part by challenging commonsense notions of small-capacity household vacuum cleaners that Sanyo made a market breakthrough with its extra-powerful Shopcleaner model.

Challenging the accepted notion that jet planes are expensive, Jim Taylor, then marketing vice president of Cessna, ordered his designers to develop a light "business jet." Nobody trying to divine the future from the history of jet aircraft up to that point would have predicted the success of that development effort. Cessna's Citation aircraft radically upset the stalemated market-share position previously held by expensive business jet and turboprop aircraft manufacturers.

Some people might choose to call these triumphs by Sony, Sanyo, and Cessna inventions. It seems to me, however, that they were not so much inspired creations of genius as natural solutions to a stalemated situation thought up by people who refuse to be bound by the status quo. Anyone, I believe, should be capable of the same kind of strategic thinking once the habit of challenging conventional assumptions has been acquired.

To learn the technique of breaking a stalemate, try making an exhaustive list of the assumptions that are accepted as common sense in your own product-market situation. Then see whether you can think up ways and means to overturn them. One way to do this is simply to ask *why* things must be done as they are now done and to challenge the supposed means again and again with the same question: Why? Let's try some mental practice to refresh our memories of Chapter 5.

**Electric light bulbs.** For a long time now, neither the shape nor the light source has undergone any change. Why must electric light bulbs be screwed or twisted in? Why not a push-in type, like a cassette tape? Why is there always a "point" light source? Why does an electric light bulb have to be too hot to touch right after it has burned out and you must remove it to replace it?

**Air-conditioners.** Both in the method of cooling and the cooling medium or agent used, air-conditioner manufacturers seem to be stuck in a rut. The Freon vaporization method currently in use is expensive; air conditioning in cars in particular accounts for 10 to 20 percent of the initial cost of the car itself. But Freon vaporization is not the only possible technology. What about the Joule-Thomson effect,* for example, which has been known for a long time, or the heat pipe, or the Peltier effect?† Why no radical departures have been

---

* This effect reveals that when a high-pressure gas passes through a porous plug or small aperture, there is a difference in temperature between the compressed gas and the released gas. This type of expansion, which is often used in industrial processes for cooling gas, might easily be adapted to automotive cooling systems.

† This effect shows that current flowing across a junction of dissimilar metals causes heat to be absorbed or liberated. Therefore, an economical refrigeration unit may possibly be developed by reversing this process.

forthcoming in this field is something I find difficult to imagine.

**Forklifts.** The traditional design of two "tines" that move up and down in unison remains unchanged, although all kinds of faults can be found with it. Why must the operator's vision be blocked when the machine is loaded? Because of the load! But why must the load be just there?

There is no end of the list of commonsense assumptions that the strategist should question. If there is no easy answer to the question: Why? then that gives him his chance. If even the experts have no satisfactory answer, it may be that common sense is blocking everyone's thinking. Remove the block, and the strategist is free to explore the feasibility of some alternative method or product design.

Once a possible alternative has been conceived and clearly set down on paper, the question of its feasibility can be answered easily, because there will be clear postulates to be proved or disproved by market research or studies of the technical development required. After that, the key to translating the new idea into a successful product or a commercial operation is basically just plain hard work.

To break through the characteristic stalemate of a mature market is not easy. But returning to basics and challenging common sense can on occasion provide the vital clue that will lead to a really decisive change. It is precisely in the stalemated situation that the high-caliber manager, who is not a prisoner of common sense but free and creative in his strategic thinking, discovers or invents the new rules of the game, using the fullest range of his talents.

## Uneven distribution of
## economic resources

According to the nineteenth-century utilitarian theory of marginal utility, economic resources consist of three elements: labor, land, and capital. Later thinkers added a fourth element: entrepreneurship. Today we have to take into consideration two further resources: materials and technology. The distribution of these two resources on a worldwide scale is strikingly uneven.

For most people, the phrase "uneven resource distribution" immediately brings to mind the oil riches of OPEC. But this is only the most conspicuous example. To achieve a more equitable distribution of valuable raw materials across national boundaries would be prohibitively expensive as well as enormously difficult for political reasons. But it would be a mistake to regard the uneven distribution of raw materials as a problem involving only the developing countries of the Third World; the biggest producers of oil and coal today are the United States and the Soviet Union.

Moreover, countries rich in scarce resources are rarely willing to sell them to other nations on a simple cash basis. Canada's western province of Alberta, for example, has massive reserves of natural gas, but complicated conditions limit its sale. Value must be added to the product by Canadian labor (e.g., it has to be sold not as gas but as methanol after conversion), and it must not be burned as fuel.

Diversification of sources of supply has been the traditional method of equalizing imbalances in raw-materials endowment (i.e., through transferring raw materials to countries which do not possess them) and of stabilizing the flow. But when the producing countries team up, as the members of OPEC have done, this solution ceases to be feasible for have-not countries, and the only remaining remedy is the application of political or military muscle. In any case, diversifying sources of supply is relatively expensive, since it makes economies of scale hard to achieve. Except where large bulk purchases are involved, it is not easy to get suppliers to lower their prices.

In general, any ironing out of national imbalances in the distribution of raw materials has become very difficult indeed. For example, Japan, whose economy is based on the export of goods manufactured from imported raw materials, is forced to buy expensive oil, gas, and scrap iron abroad. The Japanese can counter the high cost of raw materials only by striving constantly—through concentrated investment in plant at the production stage—to ensure that their products never lose their competitive edge in international markets.

In Japanese steel and shipbuilding industries, this competitive margin has so far been maintained successfully. But in other industries, such as oil refining, petrochemicals, and aluminum smelting, economies of scale have not reached the point where Japanese companies can turn out final products efficiently enough to offset their high raw-materials costs. These industries, under constant threat from international competition, are forced to choose between major investment on the one hand and withdrawal or contraction on the other, and this situation may well continue for some time.

Imbalances in the distribution of the other critical resource—technology—can be viewed from two standpoints. The first of these takes the choice of technology as given and considers technological decisions as points on a continuous spectrum between opposing concepts—e.g., basic versus applied technology, product development versus production technology, or management systems versus equipment and hardware. Here the usual question is whether the right balance between these opposites has been struck, whether the relative emphasis is right. People who approach the subject from this viewpoint often argue that basic technology tends to be neglected as compared with applied technology, or else that production technology has been favored at the expense of product-development technology in terms of the management attention and resources allocated to each area. Or again, the imbalance may be such that no strict watch is kept on the return on a multimillion-dollar R&D investment, while the cost of a project that promises a radical technological improvement may cause an uproar if, for example, a consultant or other outside service is involved, even though the expense represents only a minute fraction of the R&D budget. The principal way to correct this kind of imbalance is to locate, as quickly as possible, the technological bottlenecks that are inhibiting the company's growth and profitability.

Should a company increase its production capacity or invest more in the improvement of management techniques and staff training? Such questions don't seem to worry some managements. "Why not both?" is their reaction. "We should aim for improvement right across the board."

In reality, this is a genuine management issue involving the redistribution of resources. It is one thing for corporate management to summon all department managers and section chiefs and personally charge them to see to it that the entire organization makes every possible effort to improve. It is quite another thing for corporate management to decide which function or operation should be given priority in terms of the allocation of funds and staff. Obviously, a clear distinction must be drawn between these two types of managerial action.

Imagine an invisible storage tank suspended above the company that contains $250 million in investment funds (Figure 13–2). The strategist has to decide which stopcocks should be opened and how far in order to provide the greatest boost to the company's overall profit. How can the strategist begin to determine what will be the most effective allocation of resources?

In my experience, when a company has, say, $250 million to invest, allocations to departments tend to be made in a bureaucratic way without regard to the overall balance of the company's business portfolio. Once every five to ten years, however, the question of how much money to pour into which area must be reexamined closely. This means thoroughly reappraising the distribution of the company's resources without clinging to the criteria of the past, a process akin to that of zero-based budgeting. Hindrances to profit growth can be classified in terms of inadequacies in any of the various kinds of technology mentioned earlier, and the search for bottlenecks should be based on a diagnosis of the company as a whole.

The other approach to technology imbalances addresses itself not to questions of emphasis but to the question of which technology—e.g., semiconductor versus circuit technology, nuclear reactor versus shipbuilding technology—should be chosen in order to enhance the growth or profitability of the company as a whole. Until recently, management could reasonably think in terms of covering the waterfront. Today's changed conditions require a choice of priorities and a thoughtful redistribution of management resources.

## Growing international complexities

Radical changes that can no longer be explained in terms of East-West rivalries, North-South relationships, or

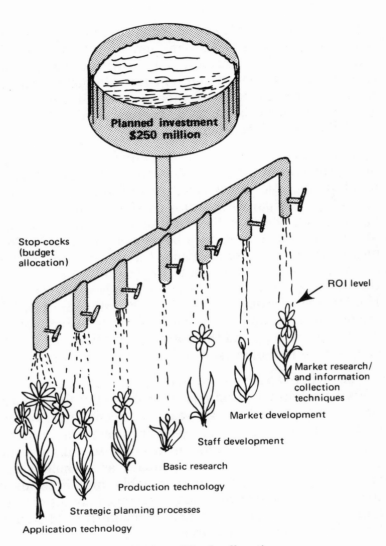

**Figure 13–2** Overall view of funds allocation.

MODERN STRATEGIC REALITIES

other simple concepts have lately been occurring on the international front. One consequence is that it has become very difficult to get accurate, reliable information on which to base long-range strategic decisions.

In 1959 Gilbert Clee, later to be managing director of McKinsey & Company, coined the term "world enterprise." The rationale of the world enterprise was the bold formula: Buy raw materials wherever they are cheapest, manufacture wherever wages are lowest, and sell wherever the products will bring the highest price. Approaches based on this concept helped the American multinationals establish themselves in Europe, to the point of raising fears among some Europeans of a virtual Yankee takeover ("*le défi americain*").

The original underlying philosophy of Clee and like-minded observers was that the narrow confines of nationality—the United States, Great Britain, Japan—were outmoded and that great corporate wealth could be amassed only by doing business with the world as a single unit.

More than two decades later, it has become obvious that the world can no longer be seen in such a simple, unitary way. Each country has its own tax system, its own laws, and its own ideology. The notion of the world as a single market looks curiously old-fashioned today. It is refuted by too many facts.

¶ U.S. semiconductor manufacturers that moved into Southeast Asia in response to the lure of low wage rates have almost all been compelled to withdraw or transfer their operations back home. Companies which stayed and invested at home have survived because the industry itself has become capital-intensive rather than labor-intensive.

¶ Japanese companies that started operating in Spain to take advantage of low labor costs have failed in almost every case.

¶ American and Japanese companies that went into Portugal to build a production beachhead in Europe before the launching of the European Economic Community (EEC) have also failed in almost every case.

¶ Most companies that have gone into South America are now finding themselves cooperating more with local capital and reducing their own share of investment in the daughter enterprises.

The world of the 1980s is a fragmented world. It cannot sensibly be regarded as a single unit for which a company can reasonably expect to be able to formulate a global strategy. In fact, without careful individual study of the more than 150 independent nations that make up the world today, effective penetration of the right overseas markets is hardly possible. These constraints barely existed during the 1960s, and, in the few instances where they did, they could largely be safely ignored.

### Irreversible inflation

The final factor in the new economic environment is the onward march of inflation. According to both Keynesian and Marxist economic theory, inflation is an irreversible phenomenon that is almost impossible to moderate by politically acceptable means. Control of inflation may of course become practicable if one is willing to pay the price of high unemployment, but given our current level of technical competence in the political and economic sphere, there is no satisfactory way of solving both problems at once. As a practical matter, this means that we had all better learn to live with inflation. For management, it means far less adequate profits, in some cases barely exceeding the cost of capital.

Consider the matter of depreciation. An inflationary environment results in inadequate depreciation. Suppose a company invests $12 million this year in new plant and equipment. At a depreciation rate of $3 million annually, amortization will be completed in four years. But when the four years are up and the company again needs to upgrade its facilities, that $12 million will no longer buy the same productive capacity. In these circumstances, so long as the same depreciation method is being pursued, the company cannot, as it should, maintain a continuous, revolving process of self-regeneration as a going concern.

Somehow, therefore, the rate of depreciation must be increased, and economists and accountants have introduced numerous techniques to do exactly that. But this will in turn increase the cost of production, and increased production costs will have to be reflected in the price of the product. Ironically, this will mean that the company is *contributing* to inflation. If competitors are better off with regard to depreciation of their production facilities, the company will be out of step with the competition if it raises its prices alone. It will be risking a loss—maybe a severe loss—of market share.

Thus, with irreversible inflation blunting the entrepreneurial will to invest, the healthy cycle of business reproduction is interrupted. That is one of the fundamental reasons why companies are going in for acquisition rather than building a new business from scratch. So many asset-intensive businesses have become prohibitively expensive to enter, against incumbents whose capital equipment costs are reasonably depreciated and whose real estate values have been pushed up by inflation. In many businesses, inflation has raised the ante for new entry and made incumbents dangerously complacent.

## Developing a
## strategic response

Before the energy crisis, the five problems we have just reviewed were hardly of any interest or concern to top management. When the crisis occurred, many top corporate managers found themselves suddenly confronted with all these problems at once and understandably became extremely confused. To grasp all the complicated changes taking place in the business environment is a tough assignment for anyone. How then should we go about tackling the still tougher assignment of formulating strategic plans?

Since we cannot predict the future, we must start from the present; and we can do so by classifying the company's businesses into four categories: replacement demand, international displacement, new economic order, and accelerated life cycle. Let's look at each in turn (Fig. 13–3).

**Replacement demand.** The first type of business consists of industries in which demand fluctuates in direct response to current economic conditions. Consumer durables provide one example. The life of a refrigerator or a washing machine may be four or five years or even more; in any case, it is measured in years rather than days or weeks. Consumers adjust their replacement schedules according to their disposable incomes by deciding to prolong or shorten the useful life of the products they have bought. If they decide to use such a product for five years instead of the past average of four, the result

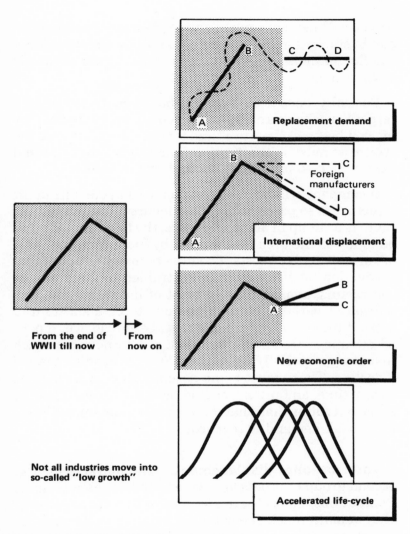

*Figure 13–3* Change in Japanese output.

will be a 20 percent drop in annual demand. Hence, durables businesses in the mature phase all exhibit quite volatile fluctuations as a result of changes in the economic environment.

Basically, once these products have penetrated into all target households and basic needs have been satisfied, the market becomes "mature" and tends to fluctuate, and the strategist must shift attention from market coverage and penetration to managing fluctuations in demand.

A company will be in no position to compete if its profit structure is so precarious that it incurs a loss every time there is a slump in demand. Hence, the first requisite will be to lower the break-even point by increasing the ratio of variable to fixed costs. The urge to invest in additional production facilities must be restrained in favor of subcontractors, again in the interest of increasing the proportion of variable costs. If there is to be a substantial expenditure on advertising, it must be spread over a period of time. Care should be taken not to hold too much inventory, especially when the market is heading toward a decline. There must be no accumulation of fixed costs at any time, and pricing should be aggressive during the surge but softer than that of the competition immediately after peak demand is reached.

**International displacement.** The markets for this second group of products have not undergone any major fluctuations, nor is there any fear of their disappearing; they remain much the same as in the past. Among this group are industries in which the costs of energy and materials have increased sharply, such as aluminum smelting and petrochemicals. There are others, such as textiles, plywood, and shoes, in which the rise in labor costs has been particularly steep.

In certain industries where competition is international, the measures I outlined in the previous section—cutting costs or lowering the break-even point—will not suffice. An aluminum-smelting company may beat rising fuel costs by constructing the most modern and efficient plant, but this alone will not restore its competitiveness or profit position in Japan.

Top management in these industries must therefore seriously consider the possibility of vertical integration. Backward integration makes sense if the profit increases disproportionately. Otherwise, a company should buy backwards but sell the raw material rather than processing it itself. Alternatively, the company might opt for forward integration by investing to gain control of the sales or distribution network.

**New economic order.** The industries in this group —typically heavy capital goods—have seen their prospects for high growth severely dampened by the rise in the price of oil and other fuels. Because of a heavy drop in demand for their products, investments in production facilities that they previously regarded as essential have turned out to be no longer necessary.

The most representative of these products is the oil tanker. Today there is a world tanker surplus. It used to be thought that tanker sales would grow even after the 1973 oil crisis, with a renewed higher price structure. But in fact shipbuilders were forced to maintain the old price structure while accommodating to a new cost structure, since fewer orders have been coming in. Seven years after the energy shock, the industry still faced great difficulties.

The electric power industry is in a similar situation. With the high cost of electricity, the growth in demand has fallen. The only recourse for the leaders in this type of industry will probably be to restructure the industry by mergers or takeovers. As we noted, the strategy of reducing the break-even point is open to assembly-oriented consumer durables industries with fluctuating demand; but with a price-cost structure changed much to its disadvantage, a company producing capital goods will not stay viable for long, even if it attempts to operate at a low break-even point. It will either have to diversify into a different field or dispose of some of its large fixed assets and prepare to survive in a period of slump with almost no prospect of growth.

Management may therefore find itself faced with a harsh choice: entering into partnership with a company that has surplus capital in an industry with bright prospects, or closing down a part of its operations and selling off those assets which cannot be used profitably. Simply holding their breath under water will not enable these companies to emerge again in the near future.

**Accelerated life cycle.**  These are the industries in which product life cycles are getting progressively shorter, a situation which calls for accelerated schedules for product introduction. Among other factors, the development of microelectronics has greatly reduced the time needed to design certain products.

Desktop electronic calculators are a familiar example. Not so long ago these had a life of one or two years. That is now down to half a year, and to three months in extreme cases. Again, there is the fashion aspect of stereo equipment today. A few years ago, when sound quality was the only object, the life of a stereo set was two to three years. Now that fashion has become an indispensable element in product differentiation, the life cycle of the stereo product has become six to eight months. More recently still, the use of microprocessors in digital watches has made the design of these products a very simple matter. Here, too, we may therefore expect a continuing acceleration of the life cycle. The same is true of peripheral computer equipment.

Product life-cycle acceleration is especially intensive in firms making use of microprocessors. For the industries concerned, it has created an environment in which companies still following the old method of starting a design from scratch and progressing cautiously from manufacturing to marketing plans are doomed to fall behind.

To cope with the problem of shorter product life cycles, many companies need to redirect their R&D efforts from basic to applied research so that they will no longer need to begin at the beginning every time a change in product design is called for. Some companies in this group are even moving to shift control over R&D from engineering or production to marketing. Others are studying computer-aided design and manufacturing (CAD/CAM) to slash the turnaround time in product design.

Top management in these industries must make the most of any market opportunity that presents itself. Conventional market theory has taught that management should invest aggressively, even accepting some losses when a market is emerging and growing, and expect profits when its products reach the growth and maturity stages. But with the type of products we are considering here, the strategist must be prepared to move in fast the moment a market appears, grow profitably with the market, and pull out just as nimbly when competitors are beginning to catch up. In other words, however technological the product, these markets must be treated like a fashion industry.

Faced with the challenges of the new economic environment, the strategic thinker should first decide in which of the four types of business just discussed his own industry or company belongs. The correct general approach—lowering the break-even point, vertical integration, restructuring the industry, or accelerating the product life cycle—should then be apparent.

# 14
# Coping with Strategic Change

Against the background of the broad economic trends we reviewed in Chapter 13, a number of important changes now taking place in the structure of world industry will influence the prospects for success of most business strategies in the years just ahead. Not all of these changes are fully understood yet; some are still unrecognized by the great majority of managers, in Japan as well as in the West, where perceptions still tend to be strongly colored by national culture and industry background. An understanding of these developments, however, can add a vital dimension of realism to the thinking of the strategist who is able to bring a global perspective to the planning task.

In my observation, at least seven major changes fall into the category I have just described: (1) a shift from labor-intensive to capital-intensive industries, (2) a shift from multinational to multilocal companies, (3) a shift in the fixed- to variable-cost ratio in several industries, (4) a shift from steel- to electronics-based industries, (5) a shift in business unit definition, (6) a shift from international to local financial management, and (7) a shift to what might be called a coordinated corporate value system. Let's look briefly at each one in turn.

### From labor to capital intensity

Traditional assembly-oriented industries—such as automobiles, appliances, semiconductors, and cameras—25 percent or more of whose total cost structures traditionally were made up of labor content, are changing. As a result of advanced production technology, automation, robot machining centers, and numerical controls, their labor content is now declining to something like 5 or 10 percent. In other words, the labor-intensive industries of yesterday are becoming capital-intensive. They no longer absorb large amounts of labor.

Managers in these industries who have failed to catch on to what has been happening find their companies suffering excessive labor costs. There is nothing to prevent them from investing to become more capital-intensive; but it will do them no good, because they don't know how to get rid of the people or how to generate enough jobs. Thus their companies are stuck with the traditional way of producing their products—a severe competitive handicap.

This is particularly evident in the contrast between Japan and the United States in these industries. Consider, for example, the way the Japanese home appliance companies reacted to what has been called the "energy shock." In 1973, the year before the energy crisis, their labor costs rose by 30 percent and their cost of materials by more than half. Normally, a manufacturer would hope to pass on cost increases of that magnitude to the customers. The Japanese home appliance companies didn't do that. Instead, they reduced the number of component items by 40 percent (they were using very little integrated circuitry at the time) and began using medium-scale integrated circuits. At the same time, they reduced the power consumption of their products by an average of 44 percent.

During this time, Matsushita, Sony, and the other four

top companies automated their color TV plants, reducing the number of line workers by as much as 40 to 50 percent and increasing production by 25 percent. At the same time, by reducing the number of product components, they improved product quality. Much the same was true of other Japanese home electric appliance makers. Instead of doing things as they had ten years earlier, they changed the physiology of the industry. The customers didn't see any price increase, because the manufacturers didn't have to pass along their costs.

As Figure 14–1 shows, the price of home appliances to the Japanese consumer has been held at roughly the same level for five years, while the general consumer price index has climbed steadily. What made this possible was the shift from a labor-intensive structure to a capital-intensive automated industry structure.

One implication of this kind of fundamental change is that traditional pricing based on experience or learning curves is becoming obsolete. Because labor content represents such a small fraction of total cost, there is correspondingly little room for improvement through learning or the accumulation of experience. Faced with a much larger proportion of fixed cost, the strategist needs to take a very different approach to the task of producing the same or improved products. Experience alone no longer enables a company to protect a superior competitive position, because its competitors are beginning to look at the industry and their roles in it in a totally different way.

Throughout the past decade, for example, Toyota Motor Company, now the world's number two car maker, has maintained its employee level at about 45,000 while increasing its throughput 2.5 times. In consequence, Toyota's productivity—as well as that of Nissan, which has taken the same route—is something like twice that

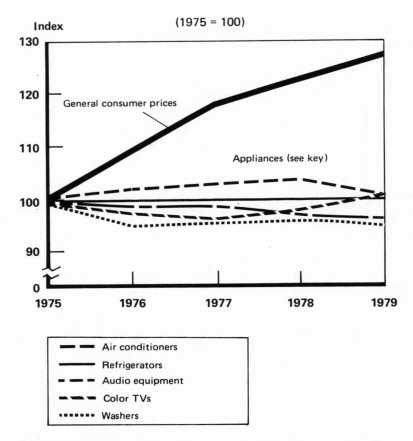

**Figure 14–1** Price index of Japanese home appliances. *(Based on data from Annual Report on the Consumer Price Index, 1979, Statistics Bureau.)*

of its global competitors, even after adjusting for differences in vertical integration (Figure 14–2). No one can so successfully overcome such a massive competitive lead of accumulated experience without starting from scratch—a zero base—and designing the plant and product simultaneously. By doing just this, Toyota has pioneered a shift

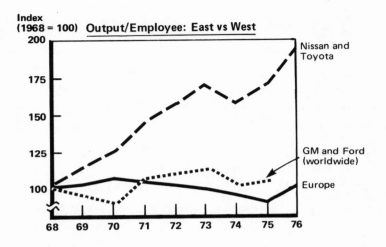

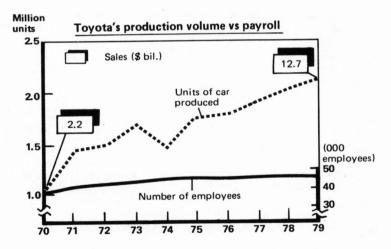

*Figure 14-2* Japanese automakers' competitive performance.

in the auto industry from labor- to capital-intensiveness.

Unlike Henry Ford, who was willing to sell his custom-

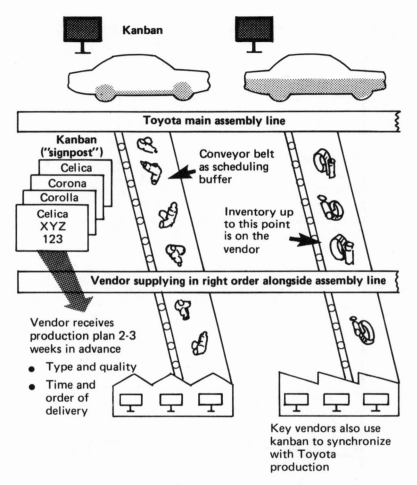

*Figure 14–3* Toyota's capital-intensive *kanban* system.

ers any color they wanted as long as it was black, Mr. Ohno of Toyota decided that every customer basically wants to have a different model and that there was no reason why that desire couldn't be met. Accordingly, he came up with the so-called *kanban* ("signpost") system, which can produce a variety of different models in what-

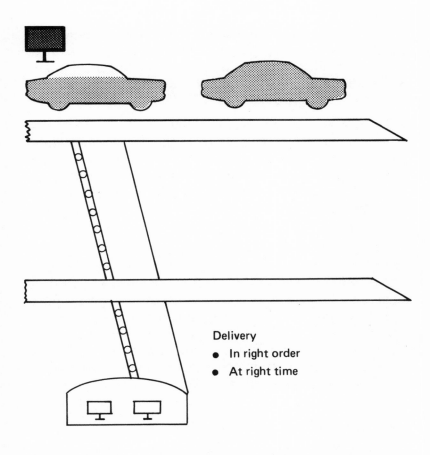

Delivery
- In right order
- At right time

ever sequence the plant receives orders from its dealers. Copies of a computer printout of the specifications of the particular car to be delivered at a given time on a given day are distributed to the vendors and posted throughout the main assembly line. To permit each car to be assembled, all the components of that particular model will be synchronized to meet at precisely the right moment at the appropriate points on the line, called "Just-in-time" at Toyota (Figure 14–3). Also, Toyota has replaced its press machine, which took hours to replace one mold with another, with a stamping machine resembling a huge lazy Susan with different molds, which can be changed over from a Celica to Corolla or other Toyota model in a matter of two minutes.

The system has obvious benefits for Toyota. First, of course, it frees the company from the necessity of maintaining a raw-materials and components stockpile; the vendors carry that inventory. Any production problem stops the whole assembly line, and top management can move to take corrective action in the shortest possible time.

But this kind of system costs money. The automobile manufacturers in Detroit have been struggling to convert a traditionally labor-intensive industry into a capital-intensive industry, ten to fifteen years after Toyota's pioneering efforts, while at the same time responding to customer needs and avoiding the loss of their employees' cooperation en route. This fundamental shift is a serious problem and one with which many assembly-oriented industries around the world are having to learn to cope.

## From multinationals to multilocals

The shift from labor-intensive industries has had an impact on developing nations. Because labor has become a much less significant element of cost over the past ten years, there is no need for companies like Toyota to seek the low-cost labor that Malaysia, Indonesia, and the Philippines have to offer.

Given Gilbert Clee's assumptions* about the homo-

---

* "Creating a World Enterprise," *Harvard Business Review,* vol. 37, no. 6, November-December 1959, pp. 77–89.

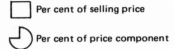

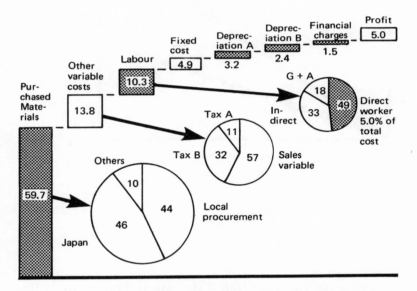

*Figure 14–4* Manufacturing economics of a global consumer electronics company.

geneity of the world and the declining importance of political boundaries and conflicts of interest between businesses and host governments, it was entirely reasonable to suppose that corporations could operate on a global scope to optimize their profit potential.

As we know, it didn't turn out that way. What has happened in the past two decades, in fact, is quite the opposite. Figure 14–4 shows a consolidated value-added tree for a Japanese company that has about thirty manu-

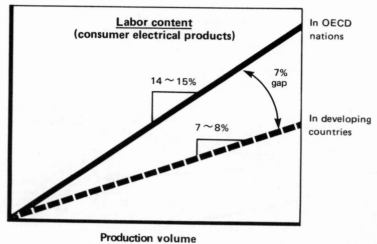

Figure 14–5 The mirage of low-cost labor.

facturing operations around the world. One thing it immediately tells us is that direct labor represents only 5 percent of the company's total costs. Even adding overhead and other variable costs brings it to only a little more than 10 percentage points. And when we lump together the labor content of all manufacturers of consumer electrical products in the Organization for Economic Cooperation and Development (OECD) nations, it comes to only 14 or 15 percent of their total costs. True, labor costs in the developing nations are only half as high, but the gap of 7 or 8 percentage points is not even large enough to cover insurance and transportation, which typically range between 10 and 15 percent (Figure 14–5).

MODERN STRATEGIC REALITIES

For most industries today, there is just no way of surmounting the economic barrier that prevents their taking advantage of the potentially lower cost of labor offered by the developing nations. This is why all the multinational corporations that used to place their operations where low-cost labor was available and focus management attention on bringing down variable cost are now consolidating their operations in fewer locations where they can secure large enough local markets. In other words, they are turning into *multilocal* companies (MLCs). Rampant protectionism further accelerates the trend. Successful global enterprises such as IBM, Pepsico, and others are each really a collection of many successful local operations.

There remains, of course, the question of the extent to which a corporation should localize and decentralize and the extent to which it should continue to exert central control over certain functions. But it is still the case that multinationals which have previously assumed a world of free-flowing resources are now having to learn how to operate as multilocal corporations, locating where their markets are and worrying more about high fixed costs of production—in other words, economies of scale and utilization in each of the markets entered. Developing countries, on the other hand, will be left behind unless they can encourage the growth of skill-intensive industries which are difficult to automate and accordingly less economically justifiable to maintain in high-labor-cost OECD countries.

Although the move toward *in situ* MLCs is inevitable, so too is the emergence of a critical change in the OECD market. What is evolving is a core of 450 million consumers who share common needs, tastes, and aspirations. Products can be developed to serve a global market—a strategy already adopted by Sony, Canon, Technics, and

Levi Strauss. These are a few of the new breed of multinationals who view the developed world, strategically, as basically a common market, but tailor strategy execution to local conditions.

## Shift from fixed-cost
## to variable-cost game

The third change I see is that traditional fixed-cost industries such as cement, textiles, plastics, and petrochemicals are, interestingly enough, becoming variable-cost industries. Most of them, because of expensive raw materials and energy, now have over 70 percent in variable costs, as compared to something like 50 percent in the past. Managing an industry of this kind today is totally different from what it was ten years ago. But those who grew up in, say, the chemical industry cannot shake off their habitual attitude toward managing their business in this new environment.

Figure 14–6 shows an example from the petrochemical industry, giving the variable cost ratios of four different first-order derivatives from crude oil at full-capacity operations. Note that over a six-year period the variable cost shot up to as much as 90 percent of the total cost. Given these economics, the strategist would therefore manage a petrochemical company almost like a trading company and certainly not emphasize "utilization," as is traditionally the case, because the waste (resulting from overproduction) in the variable cost determines life or death.

Another example of the same phenomenon can be seen in the high-value-added industries. People used to think that high value added meant high profits. The information industries in particular are characterized by high value added in terms of systems know-how, integrated circuits, and so on. Has that in fact led to higher profits?

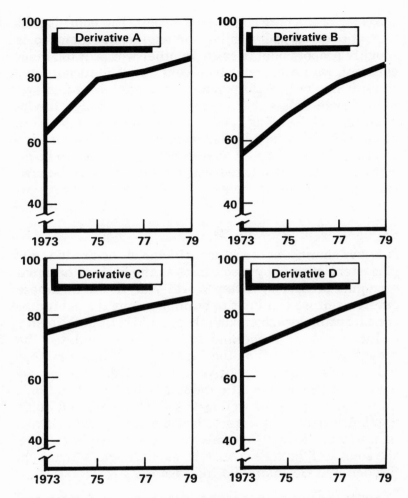

***Figure 14–6*** Petrochemical industry variable-cost ratio at full capacity (first-order derivatives).

Not noticeably. The reason is simple. In these industries top management is replacing its assembly-line workers with knowledge workers. In a sense they are simply exchanging blue-collar for white collar jobs, bleaching out the color of the blue collar, so to speak. The point is that the number of white collars or engineers employed is roughly proportional to sales. In other words, if top management wants to get 20 percent more minicomputer sales, it has to hire 20 percent more engineers and systems people unless it is prepared to alter design fundamentals, e.g., by using CAD systems. In these industries, at least, high value added certainly does not equal high profit. There are hardly any economies of scale to begin with, and these dedicated white-collar workers behave exactly like a variable cost.

## From steel to electronics

Another significant structural change is the gradual displacement of steel by electronics as the basis of national economic prosperity. After World War II, the Japanese government went all out to build a powerful steel industry. Granting low-cost loans through MITI, the Ministry of International Trade and Industry, it stimulated the growth of a 150 million-ton-capacity steel industry that today is the most competitive in the world. That success enabled the Japanese auto industry—by far the nation's largest steel user—as well as the shipbuilders and home appliance manufacturers to become highly competitive in world markets. The strategy of emphasizing steel as the source of Japan's economic strength was a triumph. Sweden and Germany did likewise.

Today, however, the emphasis is changing. Sweden and Germany, despite their steel industries, no longer have many growth industries. Most of today's growth industries, it is becoming clear, are based not on steel but on electronics. These industries, which tend to be computer-based or communications-based, are focused in the United States and in Japan, and they are becoming gigantic.

In fact, they are taking over the superior position traditionally occupied by shipbuilding, automaking, and home appliance manufacturing. Note too that in the latter two industries, the electronics content is increasing sharply. In 1983, for example, electronics will account for no less than 10 percent of the value in cars produced in Japan.

**Shift in business unit definition**

The shifting of the global economic power base to electronics creates another problem on the organizational level—namely, a new problem of business unit definition. As the electronics content of many different products increases, once-clear distinctions between businesses begin to blur. A company may have one business unit making and selling plain-paper copiers and another producing videotape recorders. But as Figure 14–7 shows, both products use the same image sensors, memories, and microprocessors, and there is a common technology across these business units: VLSI (very large scale integrated circuits). This means that management cannot, for example, safely set up plain-paper copiers as an independent business unit and forget about facsimiles, typewriters, word processors, cameras, and so on.

The reason is simply that one or more of the company's competitors that are developing computers today may enter into plain-paper copiers tomorrow. Camera producers may do likewise. In fact, all the successful Japanese makers of plain-paper copiers—Canon, Ricoh, Minolta, and Konica, to name a few—made cameras originally. Should the technology base become entirely electronic, their heavy involvement in office automation industries will enable these manufacturers to protect their traditional camera businesses. In these industries a business unit must be defined so as to encompass all possible

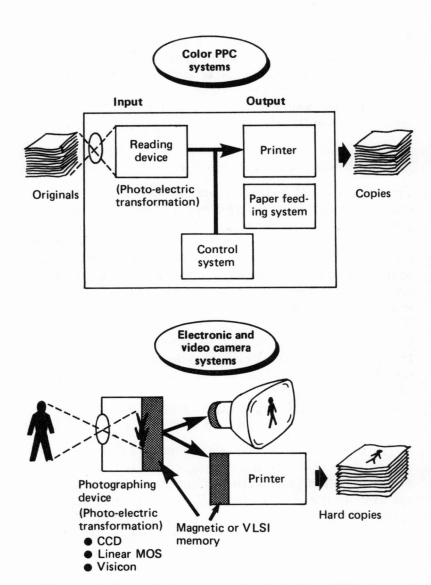

**Figure 14–7** Example of common technology across business units.

products that can be produced from critical and common technologies.

## From international to local financial management

The sixth great structural change affecting corporate operations in the 1980s is the decentralization of financial management. Not too long ago, most Japanese companies were determined to have what they called international financial management. In the quest for low-cost money, they borrowed in Switzerland, where interest costs were lowest. Today, they are having to repay those loans to the Swiss banks in Japanese yen. In the meantime, however, exchange rates have changed to their disadvantage. Although Swiss interest rates are still low, the currency disparity is making this repayment very expensive for Japanese borrowers.

A recent study suggests that the Japanese experience is not unusual. In fact, it seems quite probable that when exchange rate risks, interest rates and trends, and inflation rates are all taken into account, the result from country to country may approximate a constant. If this is so, international financial management is hardly worth the bother.

This means that a company, unless it happens to be a financial institution that can move money overnight or in a reasonably short time, needs to be able to manage its local finances very well. Thus manufacturing-oriented multinational enterprises that are unable to move large funds quickly for tax and other reasons need to provide themselves with a strong local financial base in each country where they have substantial operations. Local financing is a key consideration in an MLC model.

## From systems to human beings

The seventh and final major change that the strategist must take seriously into account is the shift in corporate value systems and the identity of the corporation.

We have all witnessed the heyday of the giant enterprise, the days when it seemed that big U.S. companies, and later big European companies, could really end up controlling the whole world. Something happened to prevent it. There has been a marked decline in the ability of large corporations to cope with the changes that confront them. In these companies, brains and muscles were separated, destroying the entire body's coordination. On one hand there were the brains; on the other there was the muscle—the people of the enterprise. They were there to make the plan a reality, to carry out the brain's instructions.

Or putting it differently, there were smart people and dumb people. The smart people were so smart that they had to spell out every detail of the corporation's strategy for three to five years into the future. They planned everything; they knew the job description of every function. Thus the dumb people never got the big picture. Instead of giving up on the smart people, they just concentrated on the boring little details that they were still allowed to control (Figure 14–8).

In Japan, where people take their career paths for granted, that separation of brain and muscle rarely happens. A person spends twenty-five years with Sumitomo or Mitsubishi as a nobody. After twenty-five years, he begins to become somebody. After thirty-five years, he is somebody of consequence. As that person moves up from one slot to the next, there is no separation of brain and muscle. There may be people with small brains and big muscles, or vice versa, but the separation seldom occurs, and the big companies stay lively and aggressive and flexible.

If we analyze the characteristics of excellent companies in Japan or elsewhere, we find that what distinguishes them is that they are human. These companies have entered what I call the new era of activated enterprise. The strategy and the organization of such a company are in harmony. Everything is geared to execution. That is how these companies achieve excellent results.

In short, the most successful large corporations today, regardless of nationality or industry, display a number of common characteristics. They offer job security, tenure-based promotion, and internal development of people instead of global recruiting campaigns. They provide endless opportunities for employee participation. They regard their people as members, not mere employees. They promote a common value system. Knowing the critical importance of the corporation's long-term well-being, they display a real commitment to the businesses they are in instead of pursuing strictly financial objectives with only the stockholders in mind.

Again, Toyota provides a good example. Toyota's suggestion box is certainly not unique to Japan. Back in the early 1950s, the company's 45,000 employees turned in only a few hundred suggestions annually. Today, Toyota gets 900,000 proposals—20 per employee on the average—per year, worth $230 million a year in savings. Even for a company the size of Toyota, that's not an insignificant sum.

Another company, Hitachi, has instituted a movement called management improvement (MI), which amounts to a value analysis of all direct and indirect work. The profit contribution from this particular set of activities in 1977 alone was about 71 percent of total profit, or $251 million.

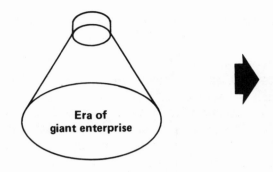

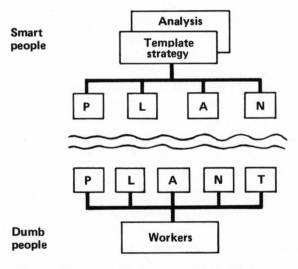

"Separation of brain and muscle"

**Smart people**

Analysis

Template strategy

| P | L | A | N |

| P | L | A | N | T |

Workers

**Dumb people**

*Figure 14-8* Excellent companies are human.

Hitachi is a $10 billion company and one of the five most profitable companies in Japan. If it didn't have its MI program, it would be one of the least profitable of its size.

When companies talk about ensuring employee participation and contributing to their people's well-being, that is strong evidence that their value systems and their

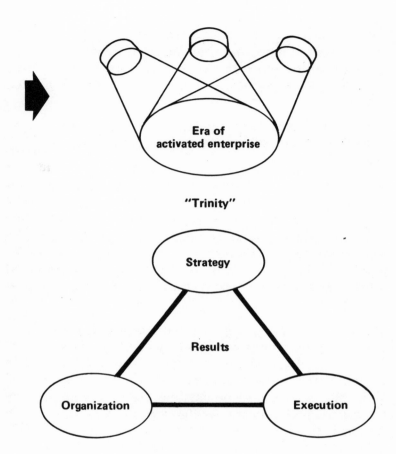

"Trinity"

whole management processes are really built around people. They don't simply put up a suggestion box and hope that somebody will come up with good ideas.

### Adding it all up

What do these seven structural changes add up to? For one thing, they mean that many time-honored management theories, concepts, and frameworks are becoming obsolete—or at least that they fail to address the dynamic changes taking place in the world today with its three strategic global regions: Europe, Japan, and the United States.

What we need today, perhaps, is not a new theory, concept, or framework, but people who can think strategically.

The strategic thinkers need sensitivity, insight, and an inquisitive mind that can't help challenging the status quo. They need a balanced perspective; they can't afford to be specialists who know only one thing. They need to be integrative problem solvers, for many contemporary problems are occurring at functional and geographical interfaces in areas where traditional expertise can be of little help.

An interesting sidelight in comparing Japanese and American companies was recently elicited by a survey of Japanese and American chief executives who were asked to name their most troublesome current concerns. The U.S. chief executives who participated in the survey said their principal concern was government regulation. In contrast, the Japanese participants typically responded, "New products" or "New businesses." A decade ago, they were worried about bad business and the task of realigning their business portfolios after the energy crisis. Today, they have sorted out these problems and apparently come to the conclusion that good businesses are not enough to sustain growth. They are worried about creating new businesses.

To come up with new ideas, new businesses, and new product lines, three basic techniques are available to the strategist. They are (1) removing bottlenecks, (2) coming up with new combinations, and (3) maximizing strategic degrees of freedom.

To review how the technique of removing bottlenecks works, let us consider a simple problem. Many pianos in Japanese homes—roughly 6 million of them—are out of tune. The reason is that tuning is very expensive; a trained tuner is required. The cost is the bottleneck, and the task is to remove that constraint. The solution: an electronic tuner. A trained piano tuner is no longer required; an oscilloscope does the job. All that is needed is a mechanic who knows how to adjust the tuning pins. The mechanic does it in fifteen minutes at a cost of $15 per year per piano. The result: a new $19 million business, 3600 new jobs, and 6 million pianos in tune.

Coming up with new combinations is very simple. One simply scans through existing combinations of things and tries putting them together mentally in different ways. How would it be, for example, if we combined these existing product lines? As Figure 14–9 indicates, questions like this will suggest quite a number of ideas for new product lines, be it beer or consumer electronics.

An Austrian economist once said that anything new in this world is a combination of known elements. Once the strategist has hit on the idea for a new combination, it is time for the analyst to step in and test it out for market potential and current feasibility.

The final technique for coming up with new business ideas is to maximize one's strategic degrees of freedom in order to achieve maximum differentiation over the competition in meeting the customer's needs. We have already discussed the concept of strategic degrees of freedom in Chapter 6. The point I want to stress here is the importance of going back to basic user objectives

**Peripheral Products**

KEY
- O  Existing
- ✓  High potential
- ?  Perhaps small
- X  No hope

| | | Packaging | | | | |
|---|---|---|---|---|---|---|
| | | Bottle | | | Can | Keg |
| | | L | M | S | | |
| Content | Regular | O | ✓ | O | O | O |
| | Light | ? | ✓ | O | ✓ | ✓ |
| | Dark | X | ? | O | ? | X |

**Approach** ➡ Analyze user segments (e.g., picnic, home party, home, restaurant) and quantify attractiveness

**Compound Products**

| | | Sub-Product | | | | | |
|---|---|---|---|---|---|---|---|
| | | Clock | Watch | Calculator | Radio | TV | Stereo |
| Main Product | Clock | | X | ✓ | O | ✓ | ? |
| | Watch | X | | ? | ? | ? | ? |
| | Calculator | ✓ | X | | ✓ | X | X |
| | Radio | O | X | ✓ | | ? | ? |
| | TV | ✓ | X | ? | ✓ | | ✓ |
| | Stereo | ✓ | X | X | O | ✓ | |

**Approach** ➡ Study the economics and assess potential market size. Do not aim at the total market, but think of 'niches'

*Figure 14-9*  How new combinations can yield innovative products.

when considering how to achieve this vital competitive differentiation. Amazingly few companies ever make a serious effort to do this: to ask what, in the most fundamental sense, the user wants from their product and whether this want might not be satisfied in a radically different and better way.

In the end, of course, a company can't meet all the users' objectives unless it is prepared to give its good products away for free. It has to consider the stockholders' objectives as well, that is, to make money. But somewhere in between there are good product ideas that will meet both sets of objectives, and some of the best of these will take a company into fundamentally different businesses.

Strategic insights often come when we analyze the forces at work in an industry with an entrepreneurial mind-set. Take home appliances, for example. We see that the competitors' technological concepts are all very similar and that the opportunities for technological innovation don't look too promising. Our insight is: Let's not knock ourselves out trying to differentiate the product itself—let's look for another way. What action does that suggest? Well, if we can establish a dominant sales and service force, maybe we can win that way. We'll protect ourselves against marginal competitors, and the undifferentiated product line doesn't matter.

Or look at audiovisual equipment. Introduction of new products is proceeding at a very rapid pace, but the products are very costly and many of them have overlapping functions. The radio in my living room has an amplifier, two speakers, and an FM tuner. The TV has the same, plus a picture tube. My stereo set has a big amplifier and beautiful speakers. All this adds up to a redundancy of functions costing probably twice what it would cost to package the best of each function and put them together as modules of a single system. In other words, these manufacturers of home audiovisual equipment are inflating their sales by a factor of 2 and are living on the redundancy. For them that represents a risk; for someone else it could be an opportunity.

Most companies never do this kind of thinking. They don't challenge the status quo. They let others define the business they are in. Their competitive posture is reactive: "If my competitor does it, I'll do it. If he attacks, I retaliate." They don't try to develop a competitive differential. And that's a fatal error for anyone but a giant, because where there is no competitive differential, the giant will always win.

Winning, or even holding your own, against a giant is possible only by doing something different. And to come up with the right "something different" takes objectivity, insight, aggressive questioning—in short, strategic thinking. Theories and concepts are subject to obsolescence; brains and thought processes are not. In today's competitive world, the mind of the strategist is an asset that constantly appreciates in value.

# 15
# Japan: Myths and Realities

In earlier chapters, I have repeatedly cited Japanese products and Japanese companies to illustrate general points about strategic thinking and strategy. It should go without saying that I have not chosen these illustrations because I think Japanese business practices hold any special fascination for Western readers. The reason is simply that although I have served as a consultant to many leading companies in Europe and North America, my experience and knowledge of Japanese business and business strategy is still probably my principal qualification for writing this book. And perhaps it was partly that background which led you to pick up this book and begin reading. In view of Japan's business successes around the world, what a Japanese business consultant has to say about business strategy might, after all, be worth looking into.

However that may be, it is certainly true that Western businessmen have been hearing a lot about Japan in recent months, and a lot of what they have heard is both mystifying and misleading. Accordingly, I want to talk here directly about Japan, expose some of the myths about Japan that have confused Western businessmen, and outline—for whatever they are worth—the realities behind some of the strategic successes achieved by Japanese businesses on the world competitive scene. Keep in mind that we will be looking at comparatively large corporations; smaller companies can seldom compete successfully on the international scene.

The real differences between the Japanese and Western business systems can probably best be considered under four headings, which we will take up in turn. Let me put them as simple assertions:

¶ The concept of the corporation is fundamentally different in Japan.

¶ To the Japanese businessman, organization *really* means people.

¶ In Japan, the government acts as the coach, not the captain.

¶ The central notion of Japanese business strategy is to change the battleground.

## Concept of the corporation

Before World War II, Japan copied its corporate system from the West. There were capitalists and laborers, haves and have-nots. The big capitalists had come into being in the late nineteenth century as a direct result of the Meiji government's determination to catch up with the strong Western nations. Most of them, including the five famous *zaibatsu* (Mitsubishi, Mitsui, Sumitomo, Furukawa, and Yasuda), took over in one way or another, at very low cost, government-initiated textile mills, copper mines, shipping companies, steel mills, and the like. Japanese companies were run much like most Western companies after the Industrial Revolution; in other words, the rich got richer, and the poor stayed poor. The laborers, exploited and lacking any job security, engaged in the usual organizing rituals. Communists were active, and companies everywhere were under pressure from strikes and demands for improved working conditions.

Most Japan watchers in the West regard the nation's current industrial system—with its characteristic features such as lifetime employment and docile labor unions—as uniquely Japanese. In reality, it was forced by necessity in the turmoil of the post-World War II days. Nearly everyone was jobless. Virtually all factories had been burned to ashes. Money had become nearly worthless, with inflation exceeding 100 percent per annum. The capitalists—the Big Five as well as many smaller companies—were broken up by *zaibatsu kaitai* because General MacArthur was convinced that some sort of military-industrial complex had pushed Japan into war.

There was virtually nothing there with which to start a corporation. Fortunately, the technology that had been devoted to the creation of tanks, airplanes, and ships was preserved in the heads of trained engineers, and some of these got together with a handful of managers from the prewar *zaibatsu* companies to start small factories producing rice cookers, clothing, and other necessities. These enterprises welcomed skilled labor but lacked money to pay wages, and so most of them paid in food, which in those days was more important than money.

In a way, these embryonic companies were more like communes than corporations. People shared their lives, hardships, and toil. If anyone tried—and some did—to organize and run a company in the old way, seeking to exploit the hungry laborers, strikes would break out. Not surprisingly, at this time the Japanese chose—though not for long—to live under a socialist government. In fact, people would have welcomed any regime that promised food.

Presently, some of these communes began to achieve a

measure of success in producing commodities for consumers and hardware for the occupation forces. But their future looked uncertain until the Korean War, when all at once they were under pressure to produce goods at more than their full capacity. They reaped handsome profits and promptly reinvested them in productive capacity as well as paying wages to the commune residents, who thereafter became monthly salaried workers.

From that point on the story is well known. The Japanese enthusiastically deposited their savings in the banks, which in turn lent quite liberally to corporations that wanted to invest for growth. Even during the growth spurt, most of these corporations kept the original commune inhabitants as their founding fathers, and indeed the sort of villager mentality that prevailed in the early days has pretty well been preserved to date.

Before any political parties, let alone national unions, were really able to organize, these commune residents had organized modest company unions in order to ensure good communications with the management and a fair share of the profits. Even today, being the leader of such a company union is regarded as a prestigious stepping-stone for an ambitious young worker on the way up the corporate ladder.

All these circumstances have been vital to the success of the Japanese corporate sector, and contemporary Japan watchers often point to them as the reasons for Japan's success. Some have even tried to copy features of the system. But the Japanese concept of a corporation, based on this commune or village concept, is fundamentally different from the Western model, which sees the stockholders as the owners of the corporation and the work force as employed labor.

In Japanese eyes a corporation is nothing but an assembly of people, each known as a *sha-in,* or member (*not* an employee), of the corporation. The stockholders are a group of wealthy and interested moneylenders. Like banks, they are simply another source of capital, willing to invest in the collective viability and wisdom of the corporation.

Many Japanese chief executives, when asked what they consider their main responsibility, will say that they work for the well-being of their people. Stockholders do not rank much higher than bankers in their list of concerns. Most Japanese chief executive officers (CEOs) are in fact employed in much the same way as factory workers, having climbed the corporate ladder starting in their early twenties and having been members of the company union before becoming *kacho* (section chiefs) in their mid-thirties.

Japan's high institutional stockholdings and relatively underdeveloped stock market can be understood only in this historical perspective. The important point is that the well-known Japanese "system," with its lifetime employment, promotion by age, and rather compliant company unions, is a consequence of the postwar communal growth, not of any preprogrammed strategy. It is a matter not of an ancient cultural heritage but of a pragmatic institutional arrangement that has now endured for more than thirty-five years.

Today the earliest of these villagers are approaching retirement age. How long the social values of the large Japanese enterprise will be able to survive their departure depends on the art of individual management. In my opinion, the ad hoc creativity of the Japanese will enable most corporations to preserve their current attitudes and customs for quite a while.

The social climate I have described, however, is peculiar to the older, larger, and more prestigious companies; it is not found in smaller enterprises. During 1979 alone, Japan saw over 17,000 companies fail, and of course there was no job security for their members. Smaller companies, which are seldom unionized, tend to hire and fire as their overall workload fluctuates. This gives the system a built-in dynamism, encouraging the relocation of labor from less to more competitive enterprises. Letting the weak companies die instead of sending in a government rescue team is yet another unpremeditated advantage of the Japanese approach.

## Organization means people

Once the historical roots of the Japanese industrial system are understood, it should be clear in what sense "organization" means "people" in Japan. But let us go one step beyond history.

Most Japanese corporations lack even a reasonable approximation of an organization chart. Honda, with $5 billion in annual turnover, is obviously quite a flexible, strategy-oriented company, capable of making prompt and far-reaching decisions. Yet nobody knows how it is organized, except that it employs project teams very frequently. In most large corporations the managing directors *(jomu)*, enjoying a very great influence on operations, are not even shown in line organization charts; they are simply footnoted as "in charge of. . . ." Many "deputies" (a title frequently given to the number two executive in a section or department) do have line responsibilities, but these are not shown on the charts. From the Western corporate point of view, such an arrangement would be confusing and unworkable. Yet most Japanese corporations can react to a changing environment much more readily than their Western counterparts.

The Western organization concept, one must remember, is copied from the military. It is an organization without redundancy, designed to eliminate all confusion in lines of command and to respond infallibly in times of emergency. It separates thinkers from doers, and information collectors from strategists. Strangely enough, the Japanese have copied this concept from Western corporations. Typically, however, they copied only the form; the substance remained Japanese, or communal.

Grossly oversimplifying, one could say that in Japan every member of the village is equal and a generalist. As far as division of labor is concerned, by mutual understanding one worker may do the accounting and another the engineering work. But managers are frequently switched around so that in theory everyone has an equal chance at the presidency. In fact, this theory verges on fantasy as far as large, established corporations are concerned today, but it does suggest the underlying spirit of the organization.

Because of this same spirit, an employee who has been handed a certain responsibility does not limit himself to this responsibility alone but rather interprets his duty as somehow more encompassing. Because he feels married to the company for life and believes their fortunes will rise or fall together, he has, in a way, a top management perspective. He knows that his colleagues are lifetime colleagues and that they all need to get along well together. Thus, lifetime employment inhibits these expansive generalists from indulging in destructive power struggles and generally guides them to seek a more sensible consensus, which is the long-term well-being of the corporation.

The Western military-type organization, on the other hand, defines jobs a priori by means of functional descriptions and tries to fit the worker to the job. The worker who best meets the job description may not quite fill all the specifications. As a rule, he will always leave something to be desired. If he is a superb performer and bigger than the job description, he will either leave the company for a better position or be promoted to a higher one. In this way, a Western corporation is never staffed with overqualified managers; in fact, it is normally staffed with below-quality managers who have yet to make the grade or, having made it, never achieve much better than mediocre performance (the well-known Peter Principle).

This is one reason why so many Western companies fail to react to environmental change as successfully as Japanese corporations, which adjust so quickly to energy crises, currency fluctuations, microelectronic revolutions, extraordinary advances in production technologies, and other major discontinuities. Such causes of competitive obsolescence typically happen at functional interfaces, further complicating the problem for most Western organizations. Consider, for example, such issues as these:

¶ At the interface between engineering and marketing and possibly between other functions as well: Should Company A install computer-aided design (CAD) to free up and reassign some engineers into marketing so as to develop product concepts closer to the actual needs of the end users?

¶ At the interfaces between R&D, engineering, and purchasing: Should Company B manufacture large-scale integrated (LSI) circuits internally to protect the confidentiality of the circuit design, or should it purchase them from outside to take advantage of other manufacturers' economies of scale?

¶ At the interfaces between international, personnel, legal, production, and possibly others: Should Company C consolidate its overseas production plants and invest in a modern production facility at a single location?

¶ At all interdepartmental interfaces: Should Company D allow each operating division to establish its own international operations, or should it provide a corporate presence to host divisional growth in each country entered?

As any experienced manager knows, there is seldom a single decisive answer to all these questions. Neither is it possible to satisfy everyone concerned. These are issues over which some managers (mainly those worried about protecting their traditional functional or operational authority) will be hurt when a final choice is reached.

Separate functional units are normally incapable of addressing such complex issues, and a company organized along functional lines will be unable to resolve them without an overall central entity to coordinate problem solving. Japanese organizations, in which each function is loosely defined and each manager's area of responsibility slightly overlaps others, are typically much better placed to identify interface issues and act accordingly without major reorganization or rewriting of job descriptions.

But this tendency is by no means unique to Japan. Similar characteristics can be seen in some U.S. and European corporations, typically those headquartered in small towns, in which key managers tend to grow with the company, rather like the Japanese lifetime employment system. According to a recent McKinsey & Company study, excellent U.S. companies display many of the characteristics of the much-praised Japanese system. The key element seems to be that each corporation, regardless of its ownership, is run in a truly democratic and humane way, as an organization "of, by, and for" the people.

Another striking characteristic of many U.S. corporations is their heavy emphasis on long-range strategic planning. For Japan, which like West Germany has no business school, it is a matter for envy that American managers seem so adept at developing rigorous and objective strategies. A Japanese planner who had just been introduced to the comprehensive computer-assisted strategic planning process of a large U.S. company, exclaimed: "My goodness, it looks as complicated as building a chemical plant!" In effect, most large U.S. corporations are run like the Soviet economy. Many are centrally planned for three to five years, with their managers' actions spelled out in impressive detail for both normal and contingency conditions. During the ongoing implementation process, each manager is "monitored" on how accurately he has been adhering to the agreed objectives.

Long study of communist and socialist regimes has convinced many observers that detailed long-range planning coupled with tight control from the center is a remarkably effective way of killing creativity and entrepreneurship at the extremities of the organization, the individuals who make it up. The experience of large Japanese corporations, on the other hand, confirms the wisdom of relying heavily on individual or group contributions and initiatives for improvement, innovation, and creative energy. In Japan, the individual employee is utilized to the fullest extent of his or her creative and productive capacity through such participative methods as suggestion boxes, quality circles, and value analysis-value engineering contests. The whole organization looks organic and entrepreneurial, as opposed to mechanistic and bureaucratic. It is less planned, less rigid, but more vision- or mission-driven than the Western organization. The basic difference is that the Japanese company starts with people, or individual constituents, trusting their capabilities and potential.

Japanese companies have many built-in devices to develop individual capabilities, ranging from language and skill-training sessions to extended sojourns in the *Jieitai* (Self-Defense Force) and in Zen temples for mental and attitudinal development. Lifetime commitment to a company and to one's colleagues acts as a very positive and sustained driving force in self-development.

Another key factor in a well-run Japanese organization is the typical career path, especially for the elite. Even the highest-ranking graduates of the best universities and graduate schools start as beginners, not experts. If they are employed in a bank, for example, they will sit behind a teller's counter or go about collecting money from private householders and "mama-papa" stores. In a manufacturing company, such graduates may start as production rescheduling clerks, working between the machinists and the line supervisors. In short, each newcomer starts where the action is and seldom where his brainpower would seem to direct him.

This emphasis on actual experience underlies the pragmatism and provides the basis for the seemingly long-term orientation of Japanese executives, in contrast to the short-term, analytical mentality of the West. Their strength lies in understanding what is really happening in the outside world among customers and competitors as well as on their own production floors.

Actually, in my opinion, many Western corporations already suffer from too much strategic planning. In the West, and particularly in the United States, there has been a tremendous emphasis on brainpower. One might call it a "McNamara syndrome" or a "von Braun complex." The assumption seems to be prevalent that because some people are more intelligent than others, it is up to the smart people to tell the less gifted—through such devices as planning processes and job descriptions—exactly what to do. The "smart" people, typically coming from law schools or business schools, enter corporate life at a pay level well above the top of the range for many middle managers. Compare, for example, the current compensation of today's typical top business school graduate with the pay of a retiring blue-collar worker or even a line supervisor.

In Japan, where tenure-based compensation is accepted as normal, a worker fresh out of college or graduate school earns—regardless of "brains"—no more than a high school-educated machinist. Western society has somehow managed to embrace equal employment opportunity (EEO) regardless of sex and race, but it seems to me that more EEO in training and promotion, regardless of people's educational and intellectual backgrounds, would be at least as important and pertinent to business performance.

In my observation, many of the problems of Western corporations are related to execution rather than strategy. Separation of muscle from brain may well be a root cause of the vicious cycle of the decline in productivity and loss of international competitiveness in which U.S. industry seems to be caught. One "blue-chip" executive I know, brought in from the recruiting market like many others, looks quite cheerful when he is talking about pricing decisions and competitive cost analysis, but his enthusiasm fades noticeably whenever I bring up his company's poor production technology and procurement practices, the real reasons why the business is unprofitable. Moreover, he seems at a loss for language to use in communicating with the work force. His elitist terminology—DCF, ROI, EPS, PPIC, price elasticity, and the like—means nothing to the straightforward people on the shop floor. They show every sign of having decided that they are indeed inferior to the elite and had better just follow orders or, when orders are not forthcoming, stick as closely as possible to whatever was laid down long ago in their job descriptions.

In striking contrast, Japanese top managers, having started out "where the rubber meets the road," never tire of reminding the employees that they, the workers, know the business best and that innovation and improvement *must* come from the *genba* (where the action is).

Not surprisingly, in such well-run companies as Toyota, Matsushita, and Hitachi, that is precisely where many of the best new ideas have in fact originated. When the Japanese say that organization is people, they really mean it. They know that a great many contemporary corporate problems fall outside the scope of organization or planning in the paperwork sense. Only active and alert organization members, working as an integrated team, can properly address and resolve them.

## Government as coach, not captain

Few observers have understood the critical importance of primary school education in Japan. From age 6 to age 12, one theme was drilled into me: how Japan could survive. Our nation—so my teachers kept telling me—has no resources, but it still has to feed over 100 million people living on a mountainous piece of land, only 10 percent of it arable, that is smaller than the state of California. The only solution to this problem, pupils were and still are told, is to import raw materials, add value to them, and export, thus earning the wealth needed to buy food from outside. We must do this or perish.

This cultural upbringing is the mainspring of the "workaholic" nature of the Japanese. People fear not to work, because if they stopped working, the country would cease to function. If they stopped exporting, they would starve. In a sense, it is almost like a robot mentality, a posthypnotic suggestion permanently implanted in the Japanese mind. People argue that because Japan is now rich, it ought to begin behaving like a big country. But this century-long psychological conditioning cannot be altered overnight. The Japanese still believe that if the work ethic should deteriorate, the country would collapse.

A population of 100 million people really dedicated to work represents a monumental victory for any nation's educational system. Although it is not explicitly stated as policy, Japan's government is indeed dedicated at the highest level to creating a people with a unified value system. That value system is shared by all ministries, from the Ministry of Education (MOE) to the famous Ministry of International Trade and Industry (MITI). My 6-year-old son, for example, is now in the last year of the three-year kindergarten program. I would have liked him to be taught arithmetic and reading, but the school's overriding emphasis has been on getting him to learn to work and play with others. This is not very different from my own upbringing thirty years earlier. Whenever I wanted to do my own thing, I was constantly reminded that the nail that sticks up gets hammered down.

Because the Japanese education system emphasizes group harmony, it discourages heroes and superperformers. No genius is permitted to skip grades or advance faster than the others. Gifted children are taught to use their extra margin of intelligence to smooth out interpersonal relationships and help their slow-moving classmates. And that, of course, is just the sort of talent required of a successful Japanese corporate executive today. Without this kind of educational upbringing, the successful features of what is known as the Japanese management approach—QC circles, suggestion boxes, and promotion by tenure, to name just a few—could not possibly work as they have done.

Western upbringing, in contrast, lays a much heavier emphasis on individualism. In the West, people are taught to state their views and defend their individual rights uncompromisingly. Few people worry very much about the effect of these values on social harmony and cooperation in a congested urban industrial society. Is it any wonder that such individualists employed by large corporations occasionally show a distressing lack of concern for the well-being of the organization as management sees it? At any rate, for Western corporations that may be tempted to copy Japanese management approaches, this fundamental cultural difference in upbringing is worth keeping in mind.

Did the Japanese government deliberately formulate this educational policy in order to support a shrewd industrial strategy? Probably not; it came about as the result of historical consequences. Before World War II, the same realization—that Japan is a small country without resources—led to a totally different conclusion: "Therefore, the nation must expand." Now that history has demonstrated that such a solution doesn't work, the conclusion has become: "Therefore, we must work harder than any other nation."

Doubtless this is far more constructive than the expansionist doctrine of the 1930s. Yet today, faced with pressures from a West perturbed by their economic successes, the Japanese are beginning to talk in terms of a trade war. They think they feel pressures from the West similar to those which emerged from the naval conferences held in London during the 1930s, when the United States joined Britain in insisting on a 6 to 10 ratio of heavy cruisers against Japan. Take, for example, two recent headlines picked at random from the popular Japanese weekly magazine *Shukan Gendai:* "American Retaliation Against Japan Is Inevitable" and "Occupation Plan of Japan by Reagan and His California Defense Industry Mafia."

The situation is by no means surprising. While trade is only one of several options that Western nations can pursue, it has been Japan's only postwar option. Thanks mainly to a constitution that bans the possession of military force, all the aggressive energies of a hyperdynamic nation have been funneled into economic and trade recovery. Sensing that its hard-won trade is at stake, Japan feels a sense of tension almost akin to that preceding a military showdown.

This is probably difficult for non-Japanese to comprehend, but it becomes more understandable after closer examination of the education system. Again, it is not a question of the nature of the Japanese per se. Japanese children of preschool age are probably among the most privileged and coddled in the world. Later, they are *taught* to behave in ways that advance the public good, *taught* to harmonize with others, and *taught* to work lest they starve. Education begins so early, and these implicit values are implanted so pervasively, that it is easy to miss the point that the work ethic is the direct result of education.

Many developing nations suffer from the lack of a work

ethic and are consequently plagued by the problems of frequent job-hopping by skilled workers. It is no wonder their behavior appears more Western than Japanese. The educational systems of most of these countries were strongly influenced by their colonial masters. Education is probably the biggest reason why the Japanese are so dissimilar in social and industrial behavior to other Asian nationalities.

At any rate, it is no coincidence that this supreme value system should be shared by MOE and MITI, two seemingly unrelated ministries. Since World War II it has been an implicit national consensus that Japan's lifeblood is trade based on value added. This is why the Japanese government, although the smallest in any OECD nation relative to GNP, has so cleverly served as coach and cheerleader in support of the nation's long-term objective: achieving economic success without a military buildup.

This shrewd coaching role played by the government has been evident from the start. In the early 1950s, for example, MITI encouraged aggressive investment in steelmaking with the slogan "Steel is the nation." What it did in terms of subsidies was negligibly small, but by openly endorsing a company (Kawasaki) that was committing itself to a rather bold growth strategy, MITI fired up the whole industry to join in a "me too" investment game. As a result, Japan as a nation has been able to produce high-quality steel at the lowest cost in the world. This competitive steel has been the underlying force behind Japan's current position in shipbuilding (50 percent of global tonnage construction), automobiles (30 percent of global units produced in 1980), and many other export-oriented industries, such as home appliances, machine tools, steel structure, and plants.

Today, MITI feels that the days of steel's dominance are about to end and is looking to very large scale integrated (VLSI) circuits to power the next industrial era. It has begun referring to VLSI as the "rice of industry," meaning that it feeds into all industries, much as rice is the basic daily food of all Japanese. That kind of open endorsement is credible enough to motivate all companies in information-based businesses to join in a massive race to develop VLSI. Many foreigners, critical of the Japanese government's "subsidies" to VLSI, mutter about Japan, Inc., or unfair competition. The truth is that the government chipped in a mere $130 million of the $320 million required by a four-year-long project. The governments of other nations might spend 10 times as much simply to subsidize microelectronics research and development in defense- and space-related industries.

Apart from rare investments of this kind, MITI has confined itself to openly endorsing vital R&D programs, mainly to develop alternative technologies for VLSI production. With this objective, five companies—Hitachi, Fujitsu, Mitsubishi, NEC, and Toshiba—formed an ad hoc cooperative in 1976, which dissolved itself in 1980 after four years of joint R&D efforts. Because they live in such a tough competitive environment, participating companies will keep investing heavily in VLSI; last year, for example, NEC alone invested close to $150 million in LSI production. None of the five can afford not to take advantage of the fruits of those four years of joint effort.

Already, products that fully reflect Japan's prowess in microelectronics—electronic cash registers, hand-held calculators, digital and analog quartz watches, cars equipped with microprocessor devices, microwave ovens, and the like—have become Japan's new export aces, and Japanese producers of VLSI itself, in the form of computer memories and microprocessors, are scoring further spectacular market successes abroad.

Once again, MITI's role with respect to VLSI is similar to its role with respect to steel twenty-five years ago: to encourage an industry critical to the survival of a nation obliged to live on value-added trade. Its financial contribution in this multibillion-dollar undertaking, however, was a mere drop in the bucket. What is interesting, and in American eyes perhaps even a bit bizarre, is the government's immense credibility with industry. When MITI publishes a long-range plan, white paper, or the like, companies will study the document very seriously and—given the highly competitive nature of Japan's free economy—will immediately make a dash to get ahead of the competition.

Not long ago, in conversation with a high-ranking official at the Ministry of Industry in a European capital, I suggested that MITI's white papers might be worth studying as a model for providing industry with implicit guidance on the reallocation of resources. The official replied gloomily: "It wouldn't work. We don't have the credibility; the industry would laugh at us. What's more, the Ministry of Trade will counter our proposal." It was only then that I recognized how lucky the Japanese had been in combining under a single ministry both international trade and industry. Here again we see reflected the supreme conviction of the Japanese that international trade must be a national way of life.

## Changing the battleground

The consciousness of the nation's poverty of natural resources and of its late arrival on the industrial scene has had a significant influence on Japanese corporate strategies. Technology, marketing skills, and capital funds have all been handled very differently from the way they would have been handled in the West. Let us look more closely at each of these resources and see what perspective they yield on corporate strategy, Japanese style.

**Technology.** Before World War II, the Japanese government took a fairly liberal attitude toward equity participation by foreign companies in Japanese industry. For example, Siemens had a 30 percent position in Fuji Electric through 1945, General Electric 50 percent in Shibaura (Toshiba) in 1910, Westinghouse 10 percent in Mitsubishi Electric in 1923, B. F. Goodrich 45 percent in Yokohama Rubber in 1917, and Western Electric 54 percent in Nippon Electric (NEC) in 1899. After the War, when most of these companies had been totally destroyed, very strict controls were imposed on foreign capital stakes in critical Japanese companies. This situation lasted until the mid-1970s, when the rules governing foreign capital participation in Japanese corporations were liberalized. During the intervening thirty years, Japanese companies aggressively borrowed Western technology through licensing arrangements so that technology would not become a critical bottleneck to their growth. It was during those days that the Japanese were called "copyists."

That is one side of the story. The other is that the Japanese are so resource-conscious that they do not themselves engage in all the activities necessary to bring products to market. For instance, while they were borrowing basic technology or design, many Japanese companies were working on other functions such as production technology, quality assurance, and yield improvement in order to generate the margins necessary to pay for the imported technology and to fund expansion of capacity. In the end, they caught up with the licensers technologically. Some of these companies, in industries such as microelectronics, steelmaking, and audiovisual home entertainment systems, are now innovating to advance the state of the art. Recently, some Japanese companies have been furnishing technical assistance to their opposite numbers in the West, reversing the traditional flow of technology.

Clearly, the habit of resource saving has served the Japanese well. Japanese industry would certainly not be where it is today if companies had tried to develop their marketing, technological, and financial capabilities all at once. They would have been weak on all fronts compared with the Western giants and unable to break out of the vicious cycle of underinvestment, lack of competitiveness, low profitability, and capital scarcity. Nor would they ever have become competitive in high-technology industries where cheap labor is no longer a decisive factor. It is therefore not surprising to see some prestigious Japanese companies contracting, as so-called original equipment manufacturers (OEMs), to supply components or even whole products to be sold under the trademark of Western competitors. These companies simply put long-term success ahead of the short-term pride and ego satisfaction of selling under their own brand names.

Many Western companies, especially the automotive giants, made the mistake of taking for granted the superiority of their own resources, especially their technological competence and engineering and marketing know-how. The automakers were exhausting their engineering competence in the effort to develop gas-turbine and solar-battery-driven cars at a time when the far more immediate challenges were to improve the emission efficiency of the traditional internal combustion engine and to reduce exhaust pollutants. Almost overnight, they found themselves forced to contend on a different battleground. By changing the design concept, relatively small, strategy-minded Japanese companies such as Honda, Toyo Kogyo (Mazda), and Mitsubishi had proved that a clean engine was possible.

This strategy of changing the battleground is a very basic habit of Japanese companies. They see it as the one effective way to compete against Western companies, with their larger markets and greater cumulative experience in technology, production, and marketing.

Today, some Japanese companies have emerged as global leaders, innovative not only in production technology but also in basic engineering and design. Moreover, recent technological advances have tended to emerge from the combination of several advanced technologies, and it is not surprising that the Japanese, with their talent for maximizing their strengths by combining available resources, should be pushing the state of the art.

Recent breakthroughs in VLSI technology, for example, have come from a combination of know-how about single crystal growth and about the electron microscope —both being areas in which the Japanese excel. Again, the home videotape recorder (VTR) became commercially viable as a result of advances in the recording density of magnetic tape and in ultraprecision machining techniques, again two areas of Japanese excellence.

Industrial robots, destined to become another big success in world markets, are likewise based on technologies —three-dimensional image sensors, microprocessors, and actuators—that are all highly advanced in Japan. Antibiotics, a large and growing field in the pharmaceutical industry, is becoming another Japanese specialty area; the basic technology consists of fermentation (soya sauce and MSG technology!) and knowledge of fungus production.

As a result of all these developments, Japan seems certain to make an increasing contribution to innovations in global technology. At long last, a handful of advanced Japanese companies can now afford the luxury of funding even quantum-jump innovation, from basic research through to commercialization. Since such innovation typically occurs at the interfaces, the flexible Japanese organization concept has therefore become an asset, especially when catalyzed by a generalist-oriented staff.

**Marketing.** In marketing too, the Japanese have avoided going global all at once. When they have an exportable product, they test it out in Southeast Asia and a few U.S. cities (notably Los Angeles) in order to learn how to market it abroad. When the situation looks risky, they ask trading companies to do the overseas marketing on their behalf, again to prevent their lack of a critical resource (in this case, marketing know-how) from becoming a bottleneck to international growth.

Such caution does not reflect a lack of interest in overseas trade. On the contrary, the company will typically dispatch a high-caliber liaison officer, usually on the CEO's orders, to such places as New York, Chicago, and Los Angeles with a specific mission to develop plans for eventual direct marketing. Many of today's top corporate executives have been on such missions at some time in their careers. The fact that the company may ask trading companies to handle their initial overseas marketing or may accept OEM deals under well-known American or European brands is likely to reflect a methodical, one-step-at-a-time approach to the long-term goal of becoming a global brand.

It is clear in hindsight that such Japanese companies as Canon, Ricoh, Panasonic, and Pentax all had an ambition to become world leaders, but each started with a trading-company, dealer, and/or OEM arrangement. Once confident of their product quality and cost-competitiveness, however, they began to address their marketing inefficiencies, gradually bypassing first the trading companies and eventually the distributor and OEM partners. Some of them still accept OEM relationships, but they will soon begin to insist on own-brand marketing as well. Dual-brand strategies have in any case been hard to administer in the United States as a result of antitrust legislation, internal administrative complexities, and conflicts over allocation of engineering resources. It was because of such difficulties that Pentax left Honeywell and Ricoh left Savin. Both aspire eventually to become global marketers in their own right.

Sequencing their marketing resources is the wisdom of these companies, whose natural human and capital resources are so scarce. But the ability to achieve and sustain consensus on a single overriding corporate goal is a major factor enabling Japanese companies to take a sequenced approach. If they were organized like their Western counterparts and staffed with managers with challenging job descriptions and associated reward systems, taking a step-by-step approach would be extremely difficult, because some managers might look embarassingly like underperformers.

**Capital.** Another instance of Japanese companies trying not to allow a weakness to block the achievement of their objectives is their high financial leverage.

In the immediate postwar era, capital was very short. The Japanese people were and are assiduous savers, but the future of most corporations was then so uncertain that they lacked the confidence to invest their savings in private enterprise. Instead, they put it into the banks, which enjoyed infallible credibility. It was through the banks that corporations with dynamic growth plans borrowed money. Freed from the need to justify complex growth plans to individual stockholders or prospective investors and from the need to worry about keeping the stock price high, corporate executives could devote all their energies to business: people, production, and products. They were convinced that by doing a superb job on these three P's they would earn the fourth P—profit—needed to repay the debt. And they were right. Had they been obliged to worry about making their financial performance look better in order to get the financing, they would have fallen into the vicious cycle of cosmetic financial management, opting for short-term profit maximization and neglecting long-term investment.

Again, sequencing was critical. Thanks to the integrative Japanese management style and governmental system, these corporations were not forced to perform before they were ready.

Another big helping hand in corporate finance came from the Japanese government's foreign capital phobia. The Ministry of Finance (MOF) and MITI, for example, in their determination to keep foreign capital from acquiring massive chunks of Japanese corporate stocks on the Tokyo Stock Exchange, did their best to encourage institutional stockholding. Although this stance is now gradually being relaxed, nearly 70 percent of Japanese corporate shares are still institutionally held. This helped Japanese companies tremendously, not only because stock prices were less affected by the transactions of individual stockholders but also because these institutional owners were, like the banks, much more understanding of the long-term strategies of the companies in which they invested. And mutual holdings within a group of companies made it impossible to exercise short-term buying and selling options.

## A success recipe

These examples amply demonstrate the way in which Japanese companies approach corporate strategy. Their long-term goal or ambition is to become global marketers, because that is what an island nation must do if it wishes to grow. But their realistic appreciation of resource bottlenecks has caused them to follow a sequential approach, taking, despite their ambition, one rather modest and humble step at a time. Their approach is designed to prevent any shortcoming from becoming a bottleneck to growth. Hence they have been led to seek a much wider range of strategic alternatives in production, engineering, and marketing.

Obviously, this approach is not without its pitfalls; many companies have disappeared from the scene in the aftermath of wrong strategic choices. Indeed, the number of Japanese corporate casualties has averaged between 13,000 and 15,000 annually. It is this tough, live-or-die domestic competition that helps Japan's free economy remain healthy.

A key aspect of Japanese corporate strategy, again prompted by the awareness of resource limitations, is the tendency to look for a different battleground on which to compete with the Western giants. For example, it was to capitalize on emission-control regulations that Honda entered four-wheel-vehicle manufacturing in the early 1970s, designing plant and car (the Civic) simultaneously so that they would be competitive in productivity with such experienced automakers as Toyota and Nissan. This approach, known as value design and zero-based production, has been one of the biggest single factors contributing to the success of assembly-oriented Japanese manufacturers.

Choosing the battleground so that they would not have to fight head-on against large Western enterprises has been the key to their success. They have sought out markets, functions, and product ranges where they could initially avoid head-to-head competition. As a result, Japanese production styles, design and engineering approaches, and personnel management philosophies are so different today that Western companies find it extremely difficult to fight back or catch up with their Japanese competitors.

Doing as the Japanese do, even if it were possible, would not be the answer. But Japanese strategic approaches, properly understood, can be a valuable source of insight for any thoughtful corporate strategist.

# 16
# Foresighted Decision Making

If you analyze the history of a successful company, you may easily get the impression that the business was created and developed under the aegis of a prophet. When I hear stories of successful entrepreneurs, I often marvel at the prophetic quality of their decision making: each decision seems so logical in retrospect. Yet at the time, the person doing the decision making probably did not use much analysis. He simply made assumptions about the future and, despite many uncertainties, succeeded in making the right decisions, one after another.

Does that mean that the entrepreneur simply gambled and won? Hardly. The process of management decision making differs fundamentally from the pure mathematical probability process involved in games such as roulette. It is true that such decisions involve judgment about uncertain elements, since the time and money available for analysis are always limited, but judgment can be supported by rational inferences. And in fact there is a discernible sequential pattern in consistently successful, foresighted management decision making. Specifically, it seems that five conditions must always be met. It is the entrepreneurs who have followed this five-step process who are known as foresighted businessmen.

1.  The business domain must be clearly defined.

2.   The forces at work in the business environment must be extrapolated into the future on the basis of cause and effect, and a logical hypothesis as to the most likely scenario must be stated simply and succinctly.

3.   Of the many strategic options open to the business, only a few may be chosen. Once the choice is made, people, technology, and money must be deployed very boldly and aggressively. By concentrating more resources in support of fewer options, the company gains a bigger edge over its competitors in those businesses and thereby improves its success rate. This is why successful and unsuccessful companies diverge so greatly over time.

4.   The company must pace its strategy according to its resources rather than going all out to achieve too much too soon. It must guard against overreaching itself.

5.   Management must adhere to the basic assumptions underlying its original strategic choice as long as those assumptions hold. But if changed conditions demand it, they must be prepared to change even the basic direction of the business.

By analyzing each of these elements in turn, we can understand the essential ingredients of foresight and see why so many unsuccessful businessmen have failed one or more of these five tests.

### Defining the business domain

To avoid spreading scarce management resources too thin, it is clearly essential not to overexpand the business domain in which investments and efforts will be concentrated. Precisely how the domain is defined, however, is the really critical point. Genichi Kawakami, rebuilder of Yamaha, makes clear in his autobiography that he made up his mind, during a trip to the United States just after the War, to develop leisure industries in Japan. Looking at Yamaha's current operations, anyone ignorant of this fact might imagine that the company had simply moved, in a fairly aimless process of horizontal diversification, from pianos into electones (electronic organs), from electones into audio equipment, and from piano cases into furniture. In fact, all these moves flowed from Mr. Kawakami's original definition of his business domain as "leisure industries," and that definition still applies today, when Yamaha's diversification has taken it into archery and skiing equipment, boats, tennis rackets, and leisure parks. There is no way of knowing the profitability of Yamaha's individual businesses, but the company's dominant market share in all those businesses which are in line with Mr. Kawakami's guiding concept provides clear evidence of the importance of defining the business domain.

In many large, diversified companies, the business domain is usually regarded, and treated, as given. This is reflected in the names of operating divisions: housing, audio, TV, microwave, and so on. Everyone takes it for granted that the TV division deals with TV and nothing else. But if this kind of labeling goes unchecked and unchallenged long enough, it can create problems.

For example, FM multiplexes for TV pose a rather interesting challenge to the existing way of defining operating divisions in brown goods companies. The FM multiplex itself is nothing but a simple device to enable the TV viewer to hear stereophonic broadcasting through the set's FM voice transmission. All that is needed to receive FM multiplex is to add another speaker to the set along with the frequency modulator. But typical consumers don't think in those terms. Their reaction will be, "Why buy another speaker for the TV? If it's a matter of two speakers, we've got the stereo in the living room. And that's got an FM tuner too." To them, it all looks suspiciously like a wasteful duplicate investment, as in fact it is.

But most audio equipment manufacturers have no TV division—and, in a typical brown goods company, the TV and audio divisions are two different worlds. In fact, in order to compete effectively with the high-quality image of specialist audio manufacturers, such across-the-board home appliance companies as Matsushita, Toshiba, and Hitachi have purposely adopted specialized audio brands (Technics, Aurex, and Lo-D, respectively). In short, although for the user home audiovisual systems represent a single way of spending leisure time, manufacturers have traditionally treated audio and video as two separate businesses. This is why the Japanese TV manufacturers' association, in trying to agree on a final, compatible FM multiplex technology, has adopted an AM/FM tuner system that is incompatible with the existing FM radio system, in total disregard of the fact that each household already has an FM tuner. In effect, the manufacturers have chosen to deceive the average consumer. To convert existing FM tuners to receive multiplex broadcasting, it would be necessary only to add a single component costing around $15, a tenth of the cost of the adapter necessary to enable an existing TV set to receive a stereophonic broadcast.

The fact that no one is yet approaching the problem of multiplex from an integrated, user-oriented standpoint offers a traditional audio manufacturer like Pioneer an unusual opportunity: purchasing picture tubes on an OEM basis and offering TV as one component of the total stereo system. The user would still have the choice of stereophonic record or cassette tape playing, but if he or she wanted to hear stereophonic TV broadcasting, a flip of a switch would connect the existing stereo system to the TV screen.

Conversely, this might be an extremely favorable moment for a traditional television manufacturer to enter the traditional audio business with a strategy based on the idea that an audio manufacturer without the capability of producing TV sets is out of date. In either case, what is crucial is the definition of a new business domain: "audiovisual systems." The traditional definitions of TV, radio, and stereo are based on hardware rather than the function—home entertainment—that the hardware is designed to serve. "Audiovisual systems," in contrast, would include videotapes, audiovisual disks, and a pulse code modulator (PCM) as well as the usual LP and/or cassette players.

The business definition of laundromats and detergents presents another interesting issue. Detergent makers today, with their large staffs of chemists, see themselves as being in the business of making and selling more and better detergents. But it is obvious when you think about it that nobody really wants to buy detergents. What the customer wants to buy is washing capability. From the user's point of view, the detergent is something that intrudes on the washing process, something that first has to be added and then has to be rinsed away, with vast amounts of water being wasted in order to get rid of it. What the user fundamentally wants—his or her objective function, as we called it in Chapter 5—is to get rid of the dirt on clothing, not to add and then remove the detergent. And a company that does not define its business along the main axis of its users' objective function—in this case, to wash—cannot claim to have a true consumer orientation.

But suppose a company defines its business domain as

getting clothes clean. Then, instead of confining themselves to detergents or other chemical agents, its R&D staff will try to come up with different methods that are within the scope of the company's defined business domain, including such physical approaches as ultrasonic waves. Such a company will not be caught off balance when an appliance manufacturer introduces an ultrasonic laundry machine that requires neither detergents nor rinsing.

Of course, the chemists will then try to counterattack. Through such retaliatory measures as the development of a detergent that cleans clothes simply by soaking, without the need for physical agitation as in today's laundromats, they will aim to eliminate such poorly defined businesses as washing machines, in which the definition of the business domain is based on means, not ends.

The first step in developing foresight, therefore, is the recognition that the only way to secure the stability of a business over the long term is to define its business domain in terms of the user's objective function and to segment the market accordingly. In the case of consumer goods businesses, the challenge is to get away from the preconceived notion of consumer needs in redefining the business domain. In the case of industrial goods, the objective function is most likely to relate to user economics: productivity improvements, rationalization, enhanced precision—whatever carries the most weight in the purchasing decision among the customers in question.

## Constructing a strategic scenario

Once the definition of the business domain has been laid down, the next important step is to identify the forces at work within that domain and summarize them concisely in a brief statement describing the relevant cause-and-effect relationships. Analysis shows that the long-term strategies of successful and foresighted business entrepreneurs can almost always be characterized precisely in a very simple and natural way. This should not be surprising, for strategy is really no more than a plan of action for maximizing one's strength against the forces at work in the business environment.

This definition of strategy is perfectly consistent with sophisticated management techniques such as product portfolio management; indeed, PPM is nothing but a very simple way of expressing what we mean by strategy. Figure 16–1 illustrates the relationship between our definition of strategy and the basic concept of PPM, which, despite its simplicity, may be expanded to apply to a very complex business system or used as a tool for managing a very large and diversified corporation.

Let us look at one or two examples of what I mean by the forces at work within a defined business domain. In Japan, car and electrical appliance manufacture are basically assembly industries. The fact that these industries are highly competitive in world markets means that the parts and component industries that constitute their hinterland are themselves very competitive. Hence, Japanese parts and components manufacturers can do business directly with their counterparts in countries where these industries are relatively weak (e.g., in Western Europe) with great benefit to both parties. On the other hand, if the manufacturers engaged in final assembly are to make direct investments in U.S. or EEC production facilities, they will be well advised to ensure access to equally competitive component supply sources.

Again, consider how social forces are changing the market environment for the food and household appliance industries. The growing emphasis on quality of life

However complex the business process and organization structure may be, effective planning requires adherence to the basic purpose of any strategy:

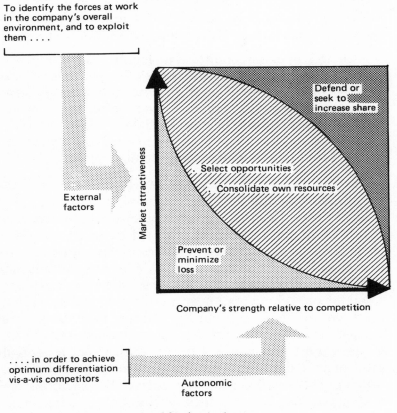

To identify the forces at work in the company's overall environment, and to exploit them . . . .

External factors

Market attractiveness

Defend or seek to increase share

Select opportunities
Consolidate own resources

Prevent or minimize loss

Company's strength relative to competition

. . . . in order to achieve optimum differentiation vis-a-vis competitors

Autonomic factors

*Figure 16–1*  Portfolio and basic strategy.

and on independence means a steady increase in the number of working wives. For the food manufacturer, this means that precooked or prepared food will increasingly be favored for domestic meal preparation. At the same time, among young working couples living within commuting distance of large employment centers, demand will grow for high-quality food (which they now can afford) that can be prepared easily but retains the quality of home cooking. The retail outlets selling these products will have to be located at suburban train stations so that the commuters can do their shopping on the way home.

Although housing conditions in Japan will not improve very rapidly, leisure time and levels of disposable income will continue to grow. Therefore, since the average family's living space will remain very limited, tremendous growth in demand can be anticipated for various electric appliances and furniture designed as modular units that can be fitted together in various configurations.

The rapid growth in Japan of fast-food chains serving medium-income families is creating an opportunity of a different sort. Existing fast-food chains set a minimum requirement for restaurant size, which in turn puts a lower limit on site area. Land prices in Japan, especially in urban areas, are astronomical by American standards. Even in good restaurant locations, however, sites too small for such chain restaurants but too large for vending machines are generally hard to sell and accordingly are comparatively low in price. This suggests that a new form of restaurant chain, based on the concept of a central kitchen in each area supporting several local outlets, would enjoy very favorable economics. By restricting operations in each outlet to food service alone, such a chain would be able to take advantage of these low-price minisites.

Or take another example. Filling stations in Japan have traditionally depended on car maintenance and servicing for a major part of their income. Now their profitability is threatened by a trend toward do-it-yourself servicing and the fact that Japanese cars, generally speaking, require less and less servicing. This calls for a redefinition of the station's function. Instead of "the place that provides fuel and service for cars," the concept might be "small convenience shopping plaza with fuel pumps and parking space." Filling stations could thus diversify into such fields as laundry, film processing, or sales of small appliances, sporting goods, home products, and plants.

In mature businesses with relatively simple products that have become hard to differentiate competitively, it would be foolish to base strategy on the assumption that the product itself has or can achieve competitive superiority. Rather, the best chance of achieving a fair level of market share or profitability comes through a strategy designed to improve the company's brand or product image and sales network.

Again, since the development of the food industry is likely to outpace the expansion of leisure and sporting facilities, there will be a gradual increase in the number of people with health problems related to overweight. Hence, a business offering various packaged combinations of weight-control products and services (such as medical and pharmaceutical products, indoor exercise equipment, health handbooks, exercise classes, and consulting services) is likely to have plenty of customers.

Managers who confine themselves to developing plans within a predefined business domain can at best improve product design or reduce costs. This situation, typical of large companies, has been called the big corporation syndrome. It is not likely to result in foresighted business decisions or world-beating products. There are thousands of business opportunities around us. All that keeps us from realizing them is the lack of a creative way of looking at the business environment and the customers we want to serve.

Here are a few useful hints for identifying the forces at work and picking out the real business opportunities when thinking through what kinds of products or services should be offered.

¶ Analyze users' total economics within the defined business domain. Because you will normally be interested in capturing a group of users having a specific common objective function, it will suffice to understand the user economics of a particular target segment; there is no need to analyze the total market. Once the target user group is identified, a thorough understanding of their total economics will help you identify opportunities for improving the user's economic benefits.

¶ If you are in a service industry, analyze the time and labor convenience of your service to the user, assuming no major change in the existing systems. Creating a new system in a service industry normally requires a massive fixed-cost investment; hence, taking advantage of the existing system and offering "additional" services is normally the best (and lowest-risk) way to succeed. Once a potential additional benefit or leverage area has been identified, it will be vital to achieve a certain threshold volume in a very short time in order to gain the advantage of economies of scale, because only after the price of the service has been brought to a generally acceptable level can you expect to expand your business rapidly. Underinvestment is the quickest way of killing a business opportunity based on a new service idea or concept, however revolutionary. The perceived benefit of a given service should always be evaluated against the price a user is willing to pay.

¶ Understand the basic reasons why the existing system is currently accepted and then challenge these fundamental assumptions.

One of the best ways to achieve competitive differentiation is to exaggerate the key factors for success in a given business. Figure 16–2 illustrates how this approach to deriving new business concepts might be applied in a service business. In trying to identify new business opportunities by analyzing cause-and-effect relationships in this way, you should pay particular attention to (1) the target segment, i.e., the customers to whom you will offer the product or service, (2) the specific nature of the service and its justification in terms of those users, (3) the perceived key factors for success, (4) the ease of competitors' entry into your target segment and how barriers to entry might be raised, and (5) the estimated size of the market for the new business and the amount of investment justified by that potential.

The success of such companies as Honda, Seiko, and YKK in establishing globally accepted brands is evidence that they did a superb job of understanding the key cause-and-effect relationships and articulating them in a succinct, simple, and logical way. In my opinion, anyone who intends to create a new business will benefit a great deal by trying to describe the intended business strategy in a brief, coherent one-sentence statement. Inability to articulate a strategy in a single incisive, natural-sounding sentence is a sure sign that there is something wrong in the strategy itself.

## Confronting critical choices

Once a strategy has been laid out for commercializing a creative business idea, there may be several available

A new large-scale service business can be developed by pricing the service below an efficient small business's break-even for the same service. Two examples:

| New business | Piano tuning | Restoring metal surfaces |
|---|---|---|
| Target market | Piano owners | All households |
| Content of the service | 15-minute tuning aided by an electronic tuner | Removal of rust, stains and corrosion from metal surfaces of products found in every home — eg., cutlery, kitchenware, bicycles, appliances |
| Market rationale | Most home pianos are chronically out of tune, because existing tuning services are so expensive | Most of these products get little or no attention of this kind once purchased, and tend to become unsightly over the course of time. Owners dislike shabby-looking possessions and would pay to have original appearance restored |
| Key success factors | . Reduced time of visits; minimum travel time<br>. Nationwide organization, recognized for reliability<br>. Periodic tuning contracts | . Carefully planned visits<br>. Cost control<br>. Technology of rust and stain removal<br>. Securing/training skilled labour to handle tools and chemicals |
| Market size | $15/tuning/year x 6 million households = $90 million/year (3,600 tuner jobs) | $5/operation/2 years x 10 million households = $25 million/year (1,000 jobs) |

*Figure 16–2* Creating a service business.

routes to implementation, making the idea of a multi-pronged implementation effort seem quite attractive. This temptation must be resisted. Successful entrepreneurs are careful not to spread their precious management resources of time, money, and people over too many areas. Rather, they typically conquer one key factor for success after another, one at a time. The principle is the same as the principle for pursuing a revolutionary technological development, especially with limited management resources. Preferential distribution of capital to the most critical areas first is the golden rule for eventual success.

It is something like betting at the racetrack. If you bet on all the horses in every race, you'll cash in on as many winners as there are races. But unless you hit a few long shots offering improbable odds, you'll soon go bankrupt. On the other hand, if you stake all your money on a single horse to win, you stand no chance to recoup if the horse loses or even shows or places. The odds of a win are perceptibly better if, after carefully considering the key factors—the horse's track history, the competition, track conditions, etc., as well as your own gambling instinct—you pick out just a few key horses. The art is to strike an optimum balance between wasteful dissipation of resources and needlessly going for broke—a balance that differs in every business situation, depending on the resources available and on the diversity and quality of the available alternatives.

Successful companies in Japan have been outstandingly effective at shifting their management attention from one function to another as the balance shifts among key factors for success in the business. These shifts, occurring as a result of changes in the environment on the one hand and changes in the corporation's degree of internationalization and sophistication on the other, offer a very effective basis for evolving a strategy step by step. Companies taking the opposite approach—simultaneous exploitation of all functions and all market regions—inevitably spread their resources so thin that they fail to establish any differentiable functional strengths and end by dissipating all their competitive momentum.

Compare this with the strategy followed by companies

like Honda and Seiko, which today are considered global enterprises. Both companies entered the low end of a market that had been established by their Western counterparts. After establishing a fund of production technology know-how and accumulating experience in designing and manufacturing these product lines, both gradually moved up toward the higher end of the market. They did not aim to cover the whole range or to blanket all customer segments. Other Japanese companies have followed a similar strategy: develop sufficient competitive power at the low end, extend the product line into medium- and high-price segments, and then gradually expand the target markets to the rest of the world.

In the early stages of such a strategy, the company in question still needs to achieve price competitiveness; hence, securing the economies of scale is likely to take precedence over building brand awareness. For this reason, such a company will be prepared to play the role of OEM (original equipment manufacturer) and rely parasitically on distributor sales rather than waste its resources prematurely on international marketing and sales. This enables it to gain, as quickly as possible, the volume base needed to generate manufacturing profits and thus become a recognized global competitor although not yet a completely functional company. Once it has attained the required economies of scale, such a company will gradually terminate its OEM supplier role and distributor arrangements and shift to establishing its own brand and its own distribution network. At this stage, the combination of competitive products and the beginnings of brand awareness may give the company some special differentiation over its competitors.

Strangely enough, every industry in which the Japanese have followed this strategy contains at least two major Japanese competitors: Sharp and Casio in personal calculators; Technics, Pioneer, and JVC in stereo equipment; Panasonic, Sony, Toshiba, and Hitachi in TV; Canon, Nikon, Konica, and Olympus in cameras; Teac and Akai in tape decks; Honda, Yamaha, Suzuki, and Kawasaki in motorbikes; MHI and IHI in shipbuilding, etc.

Even when they have expanded into foreign markets, Japanese companies continue battling each other for world leadership. Hence, global competition in these industries is to a very large extent a struggle among Japanese competitors—a struggle in which slower-moving Western competitors tend to be gradually left behind. Eventually, free competition in these industries on a global scale tends to disappear, because the surviving Japanese companies are competitively so much more powerful than the surviving Western companies that the latter are unable to close the gap, given the sociopolitical environment in which they must operate.

Should this polarization occur, it seems inevitable that a bloc economy will follow unless the Japanese can blunt their competitive zeal in order to coexist peacefully as members of the industrialized free world. Right now, the differences between Japan and the other OECD economies in design and production methods and in social and organizational flexibility almost preclude a common ground on which to base rational trade negotiations.

### Pacing progress realistically

One of the most critical elements in strategy is timing. Although its goal may be wisely chosen and its strategy correct, a company will always be constrained to some extent by the limitations of its available resources and existing strengths. Successful companies, therefore, pace their strategies accordingly. They realize that steady step-by-step progress is a much surer way of winning than an all-or-nothing dash that could end in exhaustion far short of the goal. The history of Japanese corporate casualties is studded with companies that overreached themselves in this way, mainly through ill-calculated speculations. Ataka went bankrupt as a result of its Canadian refinery acquisition, and Mitsui faces serious trouble because of its high-risk–high-return investments in Iran. These companies didn't have to take the risks they took. In every case it was deliberate. They simply overreached themselves because they were in too much of a hurry to overtake the competition.

Companies that go in for horizontal diversification based on technological commonalities furnish a particularly good illustration of this principle. Because these companies do not fully understand what it takes to succeed in the new markets they enter, their control of the market and their rapport with end-user customers is incomplete. Quite often a diversified company of this kind finds that each of its product lines is unprofitable in any given segment of the market, although the products may in themselves be perfectly satisfactory. Management fails to realize that the key to profit in a given market segment is full control of the key factors for success within that segment. To capture the key factors for success in a target segment and accumulate the business experience needed to exploit them fully takes a substantial investment of time and financial resources, coupled with a clear, step-by-step strategic scenario.

What if you have discovered a business opportunity that other companies have not yet moved to exploit, but your own resources are severely limited? In this situation, you will need to analyze your available alternatives and evaluate the pros and cons of each in a very careful and realistic way. For example, let us suppose that a company in the rapidly expanding office automation industry decides to enter the word processing business simply because of its technological capabilities in computers and paper handling.

Even though it possesses many elements of the required technology as well as the required distribution network, such a company will lack the cathode-ray tube (CRT) technology and the word processing know-how it needs for success. The gap between the company's current strengths and the identified opportunity must be filled, either through research and development or by tying in with another company that already has both the technology and the know-how.

The strategic implications of these two alternatives differ with respect both to the time required before the company can bring the product to market and to the total management resources that will be required to realize the opportunity. The company will have to allocate all its development engineers to removing the technology bottleneck, possibly at the expense of forgoing other business opportunities, or else try to be first in the market by using some other company's technology as a stepping-stone. The first option may carry a high risk, since the internal development effort could fail, but it may offer a higher potential return. The second option may offer a considerably reduced risk, but the potential rewards are also, or could be, relatively smaller (unless, perhaps, management decides to commit all its resources to succeeding in the business). The choice between the two alternatives is a function of how much risk the company is willing to take and how vital it considers the time element to be. If speed is critical for a company aiming to establish itself competitively in the word processing equipment market, it will probably pick the option that provides a time advantage.

Foresighted people and successful entrepreneurs consistently make decisions of this kind exceptionally well. For example, Matsushita tied up with Philips in order to learn electronics technology by forming a 50–50 joint venture. It also acquired a facsimile manufacturing company, Matsushita Denso, rather than developing this business within one of its subsidiaries such as Matsushita Telecommunications. These moves reflect tremendous foresight, because all these technologies may eventually be brought under the single big umbrella of office automation systems.

Again, Tokyo Electric Company abandoned the production of mechanical cash registers when it saw a once-in-a-lifetime opportunity to establish a leading share position in the Japanese cash register market by shifting to the manufacture of electronic cash registers. It entered the new segment broadly and in force, at the cost of making its own skilled machinists obsolete, because its resources would not permit it to pursue both mechanical and electronic cash registers simultaneously. Had it made the attempt, it could easily have spread itself so thin that it would never have made much of a competitive impact. Instead, by concentrating its resources, it succeeded over the course of several years in capturing better than a 40 percent share of the Japanese electronic cash register market.

In calculators, Sharp clung persistently to a strategy of exploiting liquid crystal technology to the maximum. While other competitors were pursuing rather ill-defined strategies, diversifying their products to include both LC and LED calculators, desktop printers, scientific calculators, and so on, Sharp slimmed down the personal hand-held calculator, making thinness the name of the new competitive game. Its single-mindedness paid off. Whereas forty-five companies were producing hand-held calculators in 1975, there are only two dominant makers today. The others exhausted their resources en route.

Seiko is another good example of a company conserving its resources, in this case by staying clear of competing in the low-cost digital watch market. Although Seiko was in full possession of both the digital and the analog quartz watch technologies, it concentrated on expanding its distribution network and dominating the high end of the analog quartz market rather than fighting for volume in low-value-added digital watches.

It was not until 1979, when companies like Casio entered the low-cost digital watch market in force, that Seiko finally decided to fight back against Casio and a flood of other low-cost digitals from Hong Kong. Instead of using its Seiko brand, however, the company introduced a new brand, Alba, in order to protect its pricing capability.

It is very likely that Seiko intended to shift its production gradually from mechanical to digital watches in order to use the talents of its machinists during the transition period. In the event, the speed of transition to digital could hardly have been faster. Management may have reasoned that analog technology, which absorbs more machinists than digital, would be a much more favorable competitive battleground, at least in the period of transition from mechanical watches before Seiko's machinists could be properly redeployed. This was a highly sophisticated strategy, far different from that followed by companies that market products merely because they have the technology to produce them successfully. Behind this gradual transition to digital electronics, Seiko was making a controlled, concentrated effort to establish an image, marketing, and distribution capability around the world that could withstand competitive storms in the event of major price warfare, while at the same time it was developing technological capabilities (such as double quartz) that would allow it to control a major portion of the global watch industry in the future. I believe that if worse came to worst, however, Seiko was certainly prepared to fight on any battleground. Seiko's technologies have brought to an end the centuries-long competition over the accuracy of clocks and watches and have shifted the ground of competition to design and distribution.

Or take another example. Matsushita, although active in electronics R&D, never fully commercialized its semiconductors (especially LSI and VLSI). It was in the telecommunications business, yet it withdrew early from the computer business and has never reentered the market. At the same time, however, it was developing technologies that would enable it to enter these markets at any time. Today, a company entering the semiconductor business will soon be involved in a price war with the existing semiconductor houses and may find it difficult if not impossible to make money. Still, Matsushita's integrated circuit and LSI technologies are advanced enough to give the company one of the industry's best capabilities in charged-couple devices (CCDs) and microprocessors. Using these devices, it has developed a high-speed plain-paper facsimile process that will allow it eventually to enter into the plain-paper copier business if it should choose to do so.

By combining all these technologies, Matsushita could eventually become the leader in videotape cameras, electronic cameras, plain-paper copiers, facsimiles, and industrial robots, each using image sensors and processors as well as certain actuators. Presumably the company's long-range strategy calls for entering the digital image business once industry has clearly shifted in that direction; in any case it is well positioned to capture the bulk of these markets when the time comes. The fact that Matsushita has so far refrained from entry into these businesses almost certainly reflects a well-considered strategic decision by management.

For a similar reason, GE, the world's largest manufacturer of electrical goods, has temporarily withdrawn from the semiconductor and computer businesses. This should not be interpreted as a retreat in the normal management sense but rather as the chosen means of accomplishing certain business objectives that would otherwise be out of reach. Too many companies have failed because they entered too many businesses without clearly understanding the resources required to succeed in the long term. All these cases point the same moral: Selectivity and a sequential approach are a vital precondition of successful, foresighted business decisions.

## Sticking to the basics

If a company satisfies all these conditions of foresight, it is likely to do very well. Occasionally, however, an apparently foresighted company loses out because an entrepreneurial leader forgets the fundamental reasons for his success: the original target segment and the key factors for success within it, or the assumptions on which the original business objective was based. Consider these examples:

¶ Discount stores base their strategy on the equation: Profit equals price minus cost times sales. Accordingly, they give up service and other frills and compete solely on the basis of price and volume; that is fundamentally how discounters make money. But when a discounter becomes successful and famous, the entrepreneur at the top sometimes gradually undergoes a change of personality. He begins to behave like an executive of a major corporation, and his objectives shift accordingly. Vanity pushes him to remodel the retail outlets, go in for high-style products, offer and advertise customer service, and possibly begin to pay high wages and provide employees with lavish fringe benefits—all of which mean increased costs. The equation, therefore, will no longer hold unless the erstwhile discounter either raises the price or gives up the profit. By forgetting the original success formula of his business, he imperils its survival.

¶ The success of any component manufacturer rests on its ability to supply high-quality components to the final manufacturers at a low price. When a component manufacturer has grown really large, however, it may begin to chafe at the image of vendor and subcontractor. The resulting inferiority complex may eventually prompt it to begin manufacturing final assemblies, even though it has neither the experience nor the distribution network to deliver these products to the end users.

In order to market finished consumer products successfully, a company needs to have a distribution network that will reach all the way to the dispersed and invisible users. The typical component manufacturer's traditional distribution network, however, reaches only as far as the purchasing agents of the manufacturers of the final goods. Since the entrepreneur has probably never attempted a careful analysis of current user needs, his nearest approach to competitive differentiation is likely to be a peculiar product concept that is largely irrelevant to real user requirements.

Not really knowing what it takes to sell finished products to consumers, such a component manufacturer will also find himself pitted in competition against his traditional customers, the established final set manufacturers. He may therefore be jeopardizing his core business before he can realize his ambition of becoming a final manufacturer in his own right. (Likewise, industrial goods companies are too often seized with a fatal urge to get into consumer goods businesses.)

¶ A fast-food chain's profitability depends on its ability to achieve very high turnover by limiting its menu. Often, however, competition from family restaurants will impel a fast-food chain to expand its menu, thereby reducing its turnover of materials and increasing waste. This is a sure recipe for failure.

¶ The Japan National Railway (JNR) took full advantage of its monopoly position to force the government to regulate buses and private railways, thereby denying private enterprises access to profitable routes. When the advent of the passenger car era made it possible for individual travelers to travel at the time and by the route of their choice, JNR soon lost a major proportion of its passengers and freight. Even today, however, it is still operating on assumptions that were valid only in the days when people were obliged to rely on JNR's poor service to get from place to place. As a result, strikes are common and fare increases are an annual event, and at the same time JNR's managers continue to enjoy a peaceful life at the taxpayers' expense.

¶ When an industrialized nation begins exporting plant (i.e., investing in production facilities) to the developing world, it means that over the long term, the developed country is willing to withdraw from the business in question or at least give up its previous exports to the markets where the production of the new overseas facilities will be sold. Such investments may be justified in the case of a company that has a long-term strategy to diversify into some other business, but not otherwise.

Today, however, we see almost all heavy industries looking for plant export opportunities and wittingly or unwittingly ignoring this cause-and-effect relationship. Of course, once the developing countries have installed these newer plants and increased their capacity to supply the export markets, they will not only crowd the developed countries out of these markets but will confront them with formidable new foreign competition at home.

¶ An inevitable consequence of the tire industry's shift from bias cord to the much sturdier radials, which last almost twice as long, will be a shrinkage over time in the replacement tire market. This in turn means that over the long run tire manufacturers must reduce their commitment to tires and diversify into something else. Yet instead of seriously pushing diversification strategies, most of the world's major tire producers are just sitting back and enjoying the current radial tire boom. They could hardly hit on a surer way to follow the sad example of the textile industry.

¶ Shipbuilders, power plant construction companies, and other capital goods manufacturers whose products have a long useful life ought rationally to match their production capacity to the needs of the replacement market. Typically, however, these manufacturers overbuild capacity to meet the short-term demand peaks characteristic of the growth era, only to pay the price of excessive fixed investment when demand slackens.

Not surprisingly, the current shipbuilding slump resulting from the energy crisis of 1973 has forced Japanese shipowners into a drastic joint cutback of productive capacity.

¶ As home videotape recorders penetrate consumer markets, it is clear that the sales of the 8mm motion picture industry are bound to diminish. Yet some makers of 8mm equipment are trying to prolong the life of this rather obvious loser by developing an instant 8mm film or adding sound capability.

Any successful business owes its growth and success to certain causative factors. If it loses sight of these, its growth and even its survival may soon be in jeopardy, because a business that is allowed to take its own course will inevitably fail one day. A foresighted entrepreneur does not forget for a moment which market segment he is servicing, what kind of service he is offering to what kinds of customers, or by what kind of mechanism he makes his profit. As long as he keeps all this clearly in mind, he will be highly sensitive to any changes in the market that may signal a change in the fundamental reasons for the existence of the business.

Such an entrepreneur will change the direction of his business not for reasons of ego or emotion but because of his sound knowledge and understanding of the need for such action. At first glance, it may seem that he has changed his basic course. In reality, like a hunter swinging his gun as the prey moves across his field of vision, he is simply adjusting his aim in order to hit the original mark. Nothing could be further than this from the all-too-common case of the company that loses sight of the basic assumptions underlying its success and allows destiny to control its future.

Two necessary conditions of foresight, then, are a clear definition of the business domain and a clear strategy for penetrating it profitably. But that is not sufficient. The foresighted businessman must distribute management resources economically, pace his strategy realistically, and consistently adhere to his basic assumptions. But if the world changes, he is ready and willing to change course without delay. Taken together, then, these are the necessary and sufficient ingredients of foresighted decision making—the conditions that successful entrepreneurs consistently fulfill.

# 17
# A Strategic Success Formula?

Most of us are familiar with Thomas Alva Edison's recipe for inventive genius: "1 percent inspiration, 99 percent perspiration." The same ratio holds true for creativity in any endeavor, including the development of business strategy.

Don't be misled by the ratio. That spark of insight *is* essential. Without it, strategies disintegrate into stereotypes. But to bring insight to fruition as a successful strategy takes method, mental discipline, and plain hard work.

So far we have been exploring the mental processes or thought patterns for the "grunt" part of the strategy. When we come to creative inspiration, however, our task becomes exceedingly difficult. Insight is far easier to recognize than define. Perhaps we might say that creative insight is the ability to combine, synthesize, or reshuffle previously unrelated phenomena in such a way that you get more out of the emergent whole than you have put in.

What does this all mean to the strategist? Can creativity be taught? Perhaps not. Can it be cultivated consciously? Obviously I believe so, or I wouldn't have written this book. Inventive geniuses such as Thomas Edison or Edwin Land are by definition rare exceptions. For most of us, creative insight is a smoldering ember that must be fanned constantly to glow. I strongly believe that when all the right ingredients are present—sensitivity, will, and receptiveness—they can be nurtured by example, direction, and conditioning. In short, creativity cannot be taught, but it can be learned.

Putting it more prosaically, we need to identify and stimulate those habits or conditions which nurture creativity and at the same time to crystallize the constraints or boundaries defining our probability of success.

### Sensing the limits

In my experience, there are at least three major constraints to which the business strategist needs to be sensitive. I think of them as the essential R's: reality, ripeness, and resources.

Let's begin with *reality*. Unlike scientific conceptualizers or creative artists, business strategists—as we have asserted repeatedly—must always be aware of the customer, the competition, and the company's field of competence.

Suppose you were a strategist for a light bulb manufacturer. You decided to address the challenge of product improvement solely from the perspective of customer needs, and eventually you came up with a very elegant proposal for an everlasting light bulb. Would your employer be very receptive to a formula that made the company's product line obsolete? I doubt it. Again, what would Gillette or Wilkinson do with a strategy that killed its aftermarket in blades? How could a panty hose manufacturer win with a product that did not snag or run?

In their race for preeminence in the world color TV (CTV) market, I believe that Japanese manufacturers ignored the realities of their domestic distribution structure, to their current peril. In their zeal to produce better, more reliable products, they developed color sets that last an average of seven years—nearly half again as long as previous models. Domestically, each of the three leading Japanese CTV makers—Matsushita, Hitachi, and Toshiba—relies heavily on franchised retailer outlets. These retailers are now hurting badly because customer demands for replacement and need for repair are at a low ebb.

Conversely, the Japanese dental industry, acutely aware of the long-term implications of new technology, rejected a plastic tooth coating developed in Switzerland and currently in use there. The reason is quite obvious. The coating, which reputedly can retard tooth decay dramatically, could affect employment as well as revenues among Japanese dentists and manufacturers of dental products.

*Ripeness,* or timing, is the second key consideration that the business strategist must address. Unless the time is ripe for the proposed strategy, it is virtually certain to fail.

The introduction of dishwashers in Japan a decade ago is an example of premature strategy. Not only was the average Japanese kitchen too small to accommodate a new appliance, the average homemaker was not ready for it. The attitude prevailing among homemakers, who took inordinate pride in their household chores, was that dishwashers were for the lazy or the idle rich. Today, after a decade of consciousness raising with respect to women's role, the concomitant rise in the number of working women, and the spurt of new home construction with more kitchen space, the time may be ripe for dishwashers.

Ten years ago, garbage disposal units for kitchen sinks likewise flopped on the Japanese market, but for a different reason. At that time, the sewage system in Japan's major cities was not capable of handling the additional load. This is another product for which the time may now be ripe.

Again, the makers of pneumatic shock absorbers came a cropper in the mid-1960s when they tried to repeat their success in selling to bus makers by introducing shock absorbers on trucks. The bus industry was oriented to people; truck makers cared less about driver comfort than efficient transport of goods. Today the story may well be different.

In my experience, however, more strategies fail because they are overripe than because they are premature. Think how many American and European manufacturers lost their competitive edge in international markets because they resisted automation and robotics until it was too late. Watches, autos, and cameras are a few examples that come to mind.

Word processor manufacturers who have dragged their feet in developing and marketing a unique, cost-effective product may likewise discover that time has passed them by. In my opinion, the personal computer, which can easily incorporate the same functions at little incremental cost, is well placed to usurp the word processor's role in the home market and at the low end of the office automation segment.

Video disks could prove another example of an overripe product introduction strategy, simply because too many households have already invested in videotape recorders (VTRs). In Japan, close to 10 percent of homes, representing a major share of the market for high-price-tag consumer electronic products, are already equipped with VTRs; few of these are likely to be early customers for the new alternative technology.

*Resources,* my third R, constitute such an obvious constraint that it is amazing that they should be ignored or neglected by strategists. Yet examples abound of strategies that failed because their authors were not sensitive to their own resource limitations. Take diversification as a case in point. Few food companies trying to move into pharmaceuticals, chemical companies moving into foods, or electronic component manufacturers moving into final assembly have succeeded. The basic reason in most cases has been that the companies involved were not sensitive to the limitations of their own internal resources and skills.

Toyota, for example, made the quantum jump from loom machines to automobiles successfully because the latter business was started and organized as a separate entity, able to build its own resources and develop its own core strengths. So far, however, the same company's efforts to diversify into housing have not succeeded. The reason may very well be that Toyota, instead of applying the same principle and setting up housing as a separate entity, chose instead to rely on drawing the necessary resources from its automobile organization. This has not worked so far for Toyota, because a mind-set and organization oriented toward mass production were ill-suited to respond to market needs in the eclectic housing arena.

Suntory's unimpressive performance in the beer business is another example of inadequate attention to internal resources. Despite its financial clout and an extensive distribution network, Suntory has not been able to erode Kirin's leading position in Japan's beer market by exploiting its dominant whiskey image. As a whiskey maker, Suntory's strengths are inherently oriented to the long term and thus not geared to the economics of beer distribution (e.g., multiple distribution centers and a relatively short delivery radius) or to the beer customer's buying preferences and habits.

Or consider the recent plight of EMI, the English firm which developed and launched the first X-ray computer tomography (CT) scanner. Lacking the resources to fund additional R&D and market its product aggressively, the fledgling developer was soon swamped by Siemens, GE, and Philips, who applied their ample R&D resources to extending the original CT concept rapidly to other beams and rays including ultrasonic and nuclear magnetic resonances.

Or take another example. Right now, a number of companies from different industries are jockeying for position in Japan's burgeoning office automation (OA) market. Among the entrants are general manufacturers, consumer electronic companies, telecommunications organizations, and semiconductor producers. I believe their growth in OA will be limited until they extend their current hardware orientation to include the one critical resource they now lack: software engineers. In order to gain a 1 percent share of Japan's minicomputer market, a company needs as many as 150 sales engineers.

## Conditions of creativity

Being attuned to the three R's is a necessary precondition of creative insight, but in itself it will not fan the spark of creative power within us. For that, other elements are needed. Obviously, there is no single approach that will dependably turn anyone into a superstrategist, but there are certain things we can consciously do to stretch or stimulate our creative prowess. Most important, I believe, we need to cultivate three interrelated conditions:

an initial charge, directional antennae, and a capacity to tolerate static.

Call it what you will—vision, focus, inner drive—the initial charge must be there. It is the mainspring of intuitive creativity. We have seen how Yamaha, originally a wood-based furniture company, was transformed into a major force in the leisure industry by just such a vision, born of one man's desire to bring positive enrichment into the lives of the work-oriented Japanese. From this vision he developed a totally new thrust for Yamaha.

An entire family of musical instruments and accessories—organs, trumpets, cornets, trombones, guitars, and so on—was developed to complement Yamaha's pianos. These were followed by stereo equipment, sporting goods, motorcycles, and pleasure boats. Music schools were established. Then came the Yamaha Music Camp, complete with a resort lodge complex, a game preserve, an archery range, and other leisure-oriented pursuits. Today, Yamaha plans concerts and is involved with concert hall management as well, reaping profits while enriching the lives of millions of Japanese.

If the initial charge provides the creative impetus, directional antennae are required to recognize phenomena which, as the saying goes, are in the air. These antennae are the component in the creative process that uncovers and selects, among a welter of facts and existing conditions, potentially profitable ideas that were always there but were visible only to eyes not blinded by habit.

Consider how these directional antennae work for Dr. Kazuma Tateishi, founder and chairman of Omron Tateishi Electronics. Tateishi has an uncanny flair for sensing phenomena to which the concept of flow can be applied. He perceived the banking business as a flow of cash, traffic jams and congested train stations as blocked flows of cars and people, and production lines as a physical flow of parts. From these perceptions evolved the development of Japan's first automated banking system, the introduction of sequence controllers that automatically regulate traffic according to road conditions and volume, and the evolution of the world's first unmanned railroad station based on a completely automatic system that can exchange bills for coins, issue tickets and season passes, and adjust fares and operate turnstiles. Today, Omron's automated systems are used in many industrial operations from production to distribution. Dr. Tateishi is a remarkable example of a man whose directional antennae have enabled him to implement his youthful creed: "Man should do only what only man can do."

Creative concepts often have a disruptive as well as a constructive aspect. They can shatter set patterns of thinking, threaten the status quo, or at the very least stir up people's anxieties. Often when people set out to sell or implement a creative idea, they are taking a big risk of failing, losing money, or simply making fools of themselves. That is why the will to cope with criticism, hostility, and even derision, while not necessarily a condition of creative thinking, does seem to be an important characteristic of successful innovative strategists. To squeeze the last drop out of my original metaphor, I call this the static-tolerance component of creativity.

Witness the static that Soichiro Honda had to tolerate in order to bring his clean-engine car to market. Only corporate insiders can tell how much intracompany interference he had to cope with. That the government vainly brought severe pressure on him to stay out of the auto market is no secret, however. Neither is the public ridicule he bore when industry experts scoffed at his concept.

Dr. Koji Kobayashi of NEC tolerated static of a rather different kind. Despite prevailing industry trends, he clung fast to his intuitive belief (some twenty years ahead of its time) that computers and telecommunications would one day be linked. To do so, he had to bear heavy financial burdens, internal dissension, and scorn.

All this leads me to a final observation. Strategic success cannot be reduced to a formula, nor can anyone become a strategic thinker merely by reading a book. Nevertheless, there are habits of mind and modes of thinking that can be acquired through practice to help you free the creative power of your subconscious and improve your odds of coming up with winning strategic concepts.

The main purpose of this book is to encourage you to do so and to point out the directions you should pursue. The use of Japanese examples to illustrate points and reinforce assertions may at times have given it an exotic flavor, but that is ultimately of no importance. Creativity, mental productivity, and the power of strategic insight know no national boundaries. Fortunately for all of us, they are universal.

# Index

## DATE DUE

| DEC 1 7 2010 | | | |
|---|---|---|---|
| | | JAN 3 1 2011 | |
| | | | |
| | | | |
| | | | |
| | | | |
| | | | |
| | | | |
| | | | |
| | | | |
| | | | |
| | | | |
| | | | |
| | | | |
| | | | |
| | | | |